Journal for Distinguished Language Studies

Journal for Distinguished Language Studies

The purpose of the *Journal for Distinguished Language Studies* (ISSN 1547-7819) is to provide a forum for exchanging information about teaching to and reaching near-native foreign language proficiency for teachers, learners, and professional language users. Areas of interest include research, theory, and practical application.

The *Journal for Distinguished Language Studies* has been published annually since 2003. Issue 7 is an exception to the publication schedule and is intended as a bridge issue between the early years, 2003-2010, and the current years, 2020 and later. In the early years, the *Journal for Distinguished Language Studies* was published by the Coalition of Distinguished Language Centers, which closed in 2010. The current issues are published by MSI Press LLC in Hollister, California. Subscription rates are $15/year for individuals, domestic; $45/year for individuals, international; $20/year for institutions. Subscriptions can be facilitated through orders@msipress.com or by fax/phone, 831-886-2486.

Prospective contributors should contact one of the editors, Dr. Yalun Zhou (zhouy12@rpi.edu), or Dr. Donna Bain Butler (dbutler@desu.edu).

ISBN: 9781950328857

ISSN: 1547-7819

Copyright 2020

All rights reserved. No part of this journal may be reproduced in any form without permission of the publisher except in the case of brief quotations embedded in critical articles and reviews or material already in the public domain.

The editors and publisher assume no responsibility for statements of fact or opinion by the authors.

EDITORIAL STAFF
Editor: Yalun Zhou, Ph.D.
Assistant Editor: Donna Bain Butler, Ph.D.

ADVISORY BOARD
Rajai Rasheed Al-Khanji, Ph.D. (University of Jordan)
Andrew Corin, Ph.D. (Defense Language Institute)
Rebecca L Oxford, Ph.D. (University of Maryland)
Karin Ryding, Ph.D. (Georgetown University)
Nelleke Van Deusen-Scholl, Ph.D. (Yale University)

EDITORIAL MAILING OFFICE
Journal for Distinguished Language Studies
c/o MSI Press LLC
1760-F Airline Hwy, #203
Hollister, CA 95023

Contents

EDITORS' NOTE 1

PERSONAL EXPERIENCE 3

HOW I ACHIEVED NEAR NATIVE FLUENCY IN RUSSIAN 5

FEATURE ARTICLES 15

Glancing Backward, Looking Forward: The History of the
"Level 4 Movement" and the Journal for Distinguished Language Studies 17

Rethinking the Rating Process: Solution to the
Threshold Performance Dilemma 41

Re-Conceptualizing Language Programs
to Achieve Level 4 61

To Superior and Beyond: Developing Professional Proficiency
in a Fourth-Year Russian Program 83

The Challenge of the Inverted Pyramid in
Attaining Distinguished-Level Proficiency 107

Feature Article Contributors 139

ABSTRACTS 141

Abstracts in Arabic 143

Abstracts in Chinese 145

Abstracts in French 149

Abstracts in Russian 153

Abstracts in Spanish 157

BOOK REVIEW 161

GENERAL INFORMATION 165

Books about Distinguished Language Proficiency Published in 2011-2020 167

Call for Papers 171

EDITORS' NOTE

The *Journal for Distinguished Language Studies* (JDLS) is a refereed volume that began publishing in 2003 by the Coalition of Distinguished Language Centers (founded in 2002 under the direction of Dr. Betty Lou Leaver and Boris Shekhtman). Recently transitioned to a new publisher, MSI Press LLC, this bridge issue covers the years 2011-2020 when the journal was in hiatus as a result of the previous publisher experiencing difficulty in funding publication. Following this bridge issue, the JDLS will move to regular annual publication.

JDLS is the only journal to focus exclusively on the highest levels of language achievement: that is, native-like or near-native. This level is labeled "Distinguished" by the American Council on the Teaching of Foreign Languages (ACTFL), "Level 4/Advanced Professional Proficiency" by the Interagency Language Roundtable (ILR), and Standardization Agreement (STANAG) 6001 Level 4 Language Proficiency by the NATO Bureau of International Language Coordination (NATO BILC). Descriptions can be found at the ACTFL, ILR and NATO websites.

The purpose of the journal is to create a robust international movement to promote language learning to the near-native level of proficiency. The editors seek contributions in the areas of theory, research (quantitative, qualitative, case studies, action research), and applications. The journal typically has published a balance of articles in all three categories. Published papers develop theory, share applications that work (based on the experience of those who teach that level), and report on the research needed for proper evaluation and assessment of theory and application.

The editors particularly welcome articles on the following areas:

- current status of Level 4 proficiency research in each of the four skill areas;
- teaching methods to/at/above Level 4 proficiency in each of the four skill areas;

- the role of culture in achieving Level 4 proficiency in each of the four skill areas; and
- assessment to/at/above Level 4 proficiency in each of the four skill areas.

The articles published here represent original work. They have not been previously published elsewhere or submitted to another journal or collected volume. The editors welcome questions or input any time.

- **Editor**, Yalun Zhou, Ph.D., Rensselaer Polytechnic Institute, New York, USA
- **Assistant Editor**, Donna Bain Butler, Ph.D., Delaware State University, Delaware, USA

PERSONAL EXPERIENCE

HOW I ACHIEVED NEAR NATIVE FLUENCY IN RUSSIAN

Bill Hopkins, Ph.D.

You may have long wondered how an Ohio-born fellow of one hundred percent Irish extraction, raised in the 1950s in Storm Lake, Iowa, a small farming community, could end up among other such places as in the White House and the Kremlin, interpreting for Presidents Ronald Reagan and George H. W. Bush at all the US-Soviet summit meetings throughout the 1980s and early 1990s. Or how about him almost getting his backside set ablaze while interpreting at an after dinner tete-a-tete between Reagan and Gorbachev at the Aga Khan's Geneva chateau? What about helicoptering with Bush and Gorby and interpreting on their flight to Camp David? Or how was it to do *chuchotage* interpreting for Nancy and Raisa Gorbacheva in the East Room at the INF Treaty signing, or to interpret for Ronnie and Raisa at state dinners in Geneva, Moscow, and Washington?

Was it exciting to interpret for the heads of state in the Tsar's box at the Bolshoi Theatre, listening to the national anthems and watching excerpts from *Romeo and Juliette?* Was it interesting to interpret for President Bush while he gave Gorby a private tour of the Lincoln bedroom?

Possibly you have wondered how many photos of such events were published that showed an "unidentified interpreter" in numerous print outlets including *Time, Newsweek,* the *New York Times,* the *Washington Post, Pravda* or *Izvestia.* You might even have wondered how such a fellow came to interpret a letter from President Bush before a crowd of some 225,000 on Moscow's Manezh Square at the memorial for three boys killed in the aftermath of the 1991 anti-Gorbachev coup, then negotiating through the throng with the newly arrived US Ambassador to introduce him to the recently returned Gorbachev.

Well, I can answer all those questions, because I am that "unidentified interpreter." But the response is not "Ah-shucks, it was nothin." No, the answer is that I had all those experiences and innumerable others, equally improbable and heady, because I had achieved sufficient fluency in Russian to be able to work for the State Department and serve as an interpreter for US government officials at the highest levels.

Beyond presidents and heads of state I interpreted *inter alia* for at least four US Secretaries of State, their Soviet and Russian counterparts, US Secretaries of Defense, Agriculture, Housing and Urban Development, Chairmen of the Joint Chiefs, at least nine US Ambassadors to the USSR and Russia, not to mention numerous ambassadors to the Geneva disarmament talks from 1983 until into the early 21st century.

However, the question I was asked to answer in this article was not about those kinds of experiences, but about how I managed to gain the necessary fluency in Russian to speak almost like a native and be qualified to work at that level.

Without doubt It is the rarer instance when someone with my non- Slavic background, who began studying Russian at a relatively late eighteen years of age, manages to command the Russian language to that degree.

Briefly stated, in large measure this came about thanks to old-fashioned language study, burning the midnight oil. However, over the years, there also were without doubt other contributing factors, which I want to share, since they were likewise of tremendous benefit. However, most of all, I want to reveal the one single, transformative factor to which most of all I attribute my success in achieving a command of Russian that allowed me to pursue the career I had.

Early on, aside from studying grammar, doing textbook translations, writing out and repeating declensions and conjugations, I spent innumerable hours in the language lab. While at the early stages of study I already imagined a career in the academic world, eventually I worked in the area of language support—as an interpreter and a translator—both professions naturally depending on knowing the language very well, but which also have their own particular skill sets.

Therefore, how I became a career interpreter is a closely related, but separate, story. However, from the outset, the most fundamental quest for me and certainly what drove everything else was my passion and the desire to achieve a high degree of fluency.

Nowadays the question most frequently asked me is what originally sparked my interest in Russian. Looking back, there are identifiable experiences that stand out as pivotal, because they contributed deeply to my fascination with the language and culture.

I remember during summer visits to my grandparents in Cleveland, Ohio, I had neighborhood playmates, many of whose families had come from Eastern Europe. Sometimes I would be invited into their homes for a bite to eat. The food (which

I now know to have been such things as borscht, shchav, or piroshki) was not better than my gram's creamed tuna with peas on mashed potatoes, but to me it was certainly different than our mundane Irish-American fare.

It was mystifying to me how my friends' grandmothers could speak what seemed like gibberish, but which apparently was understandable to my friends. As far as I could discern, they were all engaged in some gigantic, perplexing conspiracy. In our family the few totally nonutilitarian Irish phrases that had survived our acculturation were either comic or naughty. Meanwhile, I had no idea other than that reality itself was in all respects English-language based. I was envious of those who were privy to some other such intriguing alternative theory. I knew I wanted to figure this out.

When my mother and I would take the streetcar to go shopping in downtown Cleveland, across the steel mill flats it was possible to see the cupolas of a grand Russian Orthodox cathedral with the three-barred crosses, whose silhouette dominated the city's western skyline. For years I longed to see what that church looked like inside.

The golden opulence of Paris' St. Alexander Nevsky Orthodox cathedral, shown in the 1956 Hollywood film *Anastasia*, gave me a first glimpse into the majestic interior of such a compelling edifice. As with Vladimir's emissaries the warm candle-lit glow, the bejeweled icons, and the chants made a transcendent impression on me. Later that same year I beheld the splendor of 19th century tsarist Russia, recreated in Hollywood's version of *War and Peace*. What fascinated me above all were the exterior shots of shops and stores whose designations were written in Cyrillic letters.

The minute I came home from the movie I got out Webster's dictionary and found the Russian alphabet. I quickly concluded it contained some exotic, unpronounceable letters, but many were just like ours—except for some reason, they wrote them backward.

Many may remember that by 1957 relations with the Soviet Union were abysmal. To make things worse, that year, the USSR launched Sputnik and soon after, the dog Laika was sent into space. Those frightening and menacing events created shock waves in the US. Deep fear arose that the Soviets were beating us, not only in the nuclear field but now also in the space race.

That fear brought about something of a national policy initiative and produced a flurry of efforts in educational circles to promote Russian language studies, even at the high school level. That took place despite our practically total unpreparedness in terms of effective teaching materials or qualified personnel. However, no such campaign reached Storm Lake.

Old attitudes die hard. Foreign Language education in Iowa, where so many people had German roots, I think, had long suffered from the negative legacy that lingered after the world wars. That affected policy makers and encouraged a willingness by many to disassociate themselves from any ethnic heritage, which in turn could not help but have a negative impact on foreign language study. In Iowa one consequence of that was, for example, that efforts were undertaken to consolidate country parochial schools, which basically stamped out German-language educational institutions in the rural areas. Albeit a short-sighted and profligate attitude, such views toward potential language resources were wide-spread.

Against the complicated background of that period, imagine the dizzying furor in Iowa in September, 1959, when USSR Premier Nikita Khrushchev and his entourages actually visited Roswell Garst's highly successful Coon Rapids farming operation. I avidly followed what was for the time very extensive media coverage. Surprisingly, Khrushchev did not create the expected diabolical impression of a monster. Certainly, he could be indignant when subjected to Shirley MacLaine's can-can, but he appeared quite avuncular and affable when walking through fields to inspect the pride of Iowa, our corn. His visit further captivated my imagination, and later we learned what an impact Iowa had on him as well.

All of these experiences and impressions came together like a bolt of lightning for me in 1960 when I enrolled in the University of Iowa. Two years of study of a foreign language were required. I looked over the course offerings and immediately spied Russian. Here finally was the chance to find out so many things I had wondered about for so long. The first year's course was successful, and I continued to be interested and motivated. The second year was even more engaging.

Elena Aleksandrovna Scriabina, sister- in-law of the composer, my teacher, was a *grande dame par excellence*. Naturally, students adored her. One day in class she quite dramatically announced that Indiana University was offering a preparatory course and then a language study tour to the Soviet Union. Today that would be tantamount to being offered the opportunity to go to Mars. When my parents wondered whether such a trip would help my education, and I allowed as to how it would, they gave permission. Never having been farther east than Cleveland, but given my long-standing fascination with things Russian, I felt compelled to go. Still I was terrified.

In the 1960s Indiana University's Slavic Language Department was considered the best in the country. Its intensive summer immersion program and the study tour were renowned. All participants at every level of competence pledged to speak only Russian during the entire course. The Department was so good that in the later part of the twentieth century, I would guess probably ninety percent of those who had a career in any area related to the Soviet Union or its successor states had probably at some point studied in Bloomington.

At Iowa University I was at the top of the class. However, the Indiana program was populated with the *crème de la crème* of students of Russian from all over the country, many from Ivy League schools; moreover, many of them had Eastern European roots, so their Russian was already good. Never had I felt more like a country bumpkin, and, briefly stated, in this new environment I was quite a dunce. I did not like that.

The workshop was so intense that many of us even started dreaming in Russian. The tour itself all over the USSR was equally exhausting physically, emotionally and intellectually. Meanwhile, it became clear to me that one could say more in Russian than "Nina went to the store to buy bread." As a matter of fact, in the USSR everyone seemed to communicate in Russian, and amazingly, they appeared to have a word for almost anything. Monumental as the task seemed, I decided I wanted to speak it just as they all did.

That summer in Bloomington I found out that in this little mid-western town, aside from the university, there was also a military language school, where "critical" languages were taught. Often Russian-speaking couples would be hired to teach there, and soon grandma and grandpa would relocate to this idyllic spot. Consequently, there was a sizable Russian-speaking community there.

When I came back from the USSR, realizing how much I wanted to master the language, I decided to transfer to Indiana. That was not only because of the course offerings, but I also found out it was possible to rent a room in a Russian household. Students of other languages had their year abroad. For students of Russian in those days such an option was unheard of. Living with a Russian-speaking family, constantly in the authentic linguistic milieu, I thought could be close second. It was.

Moreover, when students like myself demonstrated interest, they were warmly welcomed into the Russian community. I continued classroom studies, but living with native speakers and becoming part of the emigre community gave me a second youth and adolescence—in Russian. This experience was invaluable.

Another linchpin in my developing fluency was a psycholinguistic element. It became indispensable for me always to have a close friend who was a native speaker with whom I spoke only Russian. Such relationships allowed me to feel I somehow had a "right" to speak the language, and with such friends I was not afraid to go beyond my linguistic comfort zone. They willingly corrected all my numerous, frequent mistakes. Since Bloomington days I have consistently maintained close friendships with many native speakers, and thanks to all of them I also was able to improve and maintain fluency. That is still true.

Graduate school was stimulating but stressful. We studied literature and linguistics, and I will have much more to say about one particular linguistics course later, because it was absolutely transformative. Meanwhile, I was assigned ever higher-level teaching assistantships, and I loved teaching. Nothing helps you learn a subject so much as teaching it does. I had continuing academic contact with the language through teaching, and I also improved my facility with Russian through ongoing interaction with the many native speakers.

After passing doctoral exams, participating in a teachers' summer exchange program at Moscow University, a Fulbright-year in Europe doing dissertation research (the topic was "pornography in 18th and 19th century Russia," so research in the Soviet Union was unthinkable), and teaching at Middlebury College for a year and a summer, I moved to Washington, D.C., to have access to the Library of Congress' Slavic collection and to finish dissertation research.

One day on a D.C. street I ran into an acquaintance who had participated in that very first study trip I had taken to the USSR in 1962. By this time, he was in the diplomatic corps, and he wondered whether I had kept up my Russian. When it turned out that I had, he advised me to get in touch with Language Services at the State Department to take an interpreting exam. State was looking to increase its stable of contract Russian interpreters.

To my surprise, I passed. Then, a new chapter in my life began. I was given contract interpreting assignments to travel with Soviet delegations around the US or with US delegations in the Soviet Union. The only previous interpreting experiences I had had were in the medical area, at an STD examination on a Soviet steamship going from Istanbul to Yalta and in Vermont at an emergency spinal tap. Despite my inexperience as an interpreter and the fact that every day seemed like a final exam, I somehow always managed to handle the interpreting demands of the job. I studied conscientiously for all assignments, and thanks to all those Russian courses and grad school, I knew how to cram and memorize lots of material under deadlines.

The technical subject matter and requisite vocabulary went miles beyond the genteel literary and kitchen Russian with which I had become proficient up until then. For example, subjects ranged from fast breeder reactors, to waste water treatment, to construction in seismic zones, to doing rounds with oncologists at Sloan Kettering. These interpreting trips gave me substantial practice in diverse fields interacting with numerous native speakers, and naturally that also expanded my Russian fluency immeasurably.

Eventually, I began to alternate between interpreting assignments and periods of working on the dissertation. When I finally defended it, few jobs were available in academe. Meanwhile, I realized that, perhaps by default, I had become a professional interpreter.

The State Department began sending me to Geneva, and I became a regular at the arms talks. In a couple years I was asked to become a staff interpreter. Undoubtedly, the Geneva years also helped my Russian tremendously. I learned the language of diplomatic negotiations and the arcane technical jargon that goes into working out arms control treaties. Moreover, I also did considerable translating of official documents, where the demand for exactitude was beyond beneficial.

However, because of unforeseen circumstances, it was sometimes difficult to believe I was going to be able to improve my Russian any further. For example, the dream Geneva job was a mixed blessing in that respect. As the years passed, during certain periods, it became increasingly difficult simply to interact normally with

Russia speakers because of security clearances and non-fraternization rules. As a professional government interpreter working at the highest diplomatic levels but a non-native speaker, it was imperative for me constantly to get practice, maintain and improve my Russian. However, I found myself in the absurd situation of not being allowed to use the language very much other than at work. At the very early days of my studies with few native speakers to be found, Russian had been quite inaccessible for me, almost a "secret" language. Bizarre as it was, when I became an interpreter for the State Department the opportunity to use it outside of work became almost forbidden. Nonetheless, despite all of those sorts of obstacles, over the years I persevered and somehow maintained my fluency.

The pinnacle of my relationship with Russian came in 2011, when I was invited to do an encore performance at the Moscow Embassy as the Ambassador's interpreter. I had served in that capacity for two years after the 1991 coup. This time I joined the foreign service and went to Moscow as the Ambassador's interpreter and also head of the Embassy's language support operation. I stayed at that job for five years, and it gave me an opportunity to utilize everything I had ever learned over all the years. At last I was in a milieu where I was constantly, everywhere, surrounded by the living language. The satisfaction I derived from using the language in my daily life, even going to the grocery store or cleaners, and being successful and respected in my job, especially by the Russian speakers at the Embassy, made all the efforts I had invested in mastering Russian over all those years absolutely worth it. There could not have been a more gratifying experience for me.

For this article, I was asked to recount how I, with no Russian background and having started to study the language rather late, was able to achieve near native fluency. As you might understand by now, the implication of that question is highly flattering to someone like myself, who wanted and worked so intensely to achieve that goal. However, I have to reject the notion that I have near native fluency. No one knows better than I the lacunae in my knowledge. Every day I still encounter new words or constructions that I have to look up or ask a native speaker to explain to me. I will always have an accent.

However, I do unabashedly claim to have achieved a great degree of facility with the language, which allowed me to enjoy quite a unique and exciting high-level career. I have given this omnibus tour of my almost life-long interest and passion for the Russian language and culture and perhaps even too detailed a description of my professional endeavors in order to demonstrate the magnitude of my efforts.

Beyond that I have also recounted details of this story to substantiate and to give gravitas to what was, notwithstanding absolutely all the other invaluable contributing factors, the single most important element to my success in achieving this kind of fluency.

I can unequivocally state that a linguistics course on the structure of Russian, which I took in second-year grad school, was the most determinative factor in my pursuit of achieving fluency. If it were not for that course, I do not believe I would ever have been able to advance beyond where I was at that time, and certainly there would not have been any life-long language career like the one I had.

Notwithstanding all my hard work and efforts, Russian had always remained for me a vast compendium of exceptions to rules that a student could memorize or not or perhaps use often enough sometimes to say something correctly. There were no alternatives. Despite the heroic efforts of our many wonderful, dedicated teachers, the explanations they gave often required accepting an answer on faith ("My tak govorim." "That is how we say it.") Understanding was not a requisite.

When I finally became familiar with Roman Jakobson's structural description of Russian (developed by the Prague school of linguists in the 1920s), I was nearly physically bowled over when I realized that far from being some hodge-podge, the language was almost a fiendishly or divinely organized *system*, and every part of it worked perfectly with every other part. Even the multitude of mystifying exceptions became explicable.

What arithmetic was to Euclid, drawing to DaVinci, scales to Horowitz, from then on structural linguistics has been and is to me. Suddenly, everything made perfect sense. How I regret not having been privy to that information earlier on in my study. Had that been the case, how much more effortless everything would have been to learn and assimilate. Up until then whatever success I had had was thanks to brute memorization and repetition, hard work. I had resigned myself to the fact that I would go to my grave never understanding certain most elementary things about the language. If that had continued to be the case, I never could have gone on to develop the fluency I ultimately achieved. After that course everything I learned was incorporated into the framework of that transformative course on the structure of Russian. It was a force multiplier on steroids. For example, gone was the necessity for pages of addenda in text books showing paradigms of various adjectival or noun declensions. Crazy verb conjugations were shown to make absolute sense. Imagine, the fundamental descriptions of declension and conjugations could be reduced to and presented in probably five pages. It took some effort to master that material, but certainly not years.

I have been around studying and teaching Russian long enough to have gone through many changing approaches and philosophies as to what is most effective. I also appreciate all the work that has been done on differing teaching and learning styles, and I respect that. However, whenever and wherever I have advocated for teaching structure, I have always encountered push back, from colleagues and students alike.

I firmly believe the structure of the Russian language, while it is ultimately ingeniously straightforward is nonetheless too complex for an ordinary learner beyond the age of thirteen or so, if not blessed with some extraordinary language learning ability, to intuit independently and internalize it as a child does. Even in the case of some prodigy, knowing the structure of the language would expedite the learning process.

Consequently, on the basis of my experience and speaking from the perspective of all these years, it would be my fondest wish that every student who studies Russian should have the opportunity to take a linguistics course in structure early on. No one should mistakenly think that it would be a course in speaking the language. It would be a linguistics course, *about* the language. Patience and hard work would be necessary, because some of the concepts in structure are unfamiliar. However, knowledge of Russia structure would make everything else in the long-term process of learning the language itself immeasurably easier. To gain fluency it is totally worth the effort.

This recounts my experience. In answering the question of fluency, I considered everything that went into that effort. That examination has led to my profound conviction that that one course was decisive to my success. This is the "how-I-did-it" response I want to share with everyone. Having the benefit of knowing Russian structure was the key to my personal success.

FEATURE ARTICLES

Glancing Backward, Looking Forward: The History of the "Level 4 Movement" and the Journal for Distinguished Language Studies

Betty Lou Leaver

Abstract

This article looks at what has been informally called the Level-4 Movement from an historical perspective: beginning in the mid-1980s, reaching its greatest achievements circa 2010, and subsiding slowly over the following ten years. Now, a small group of experienced and interested teachers, learners, and administrators are re-engaging. The mechanisms of socializing the movement—an annual conference, publication of conference proceedings, and the annual articles in the Journal for Distinguished Language Studies—are all part of an international effort associated with the Coalition of Distinguished Language Centers (CDLC), out of sight with the closing of the CDLC in 2010. This article suggests that from the embers can rise a phoenix, pointing to places where the coals have remained hot and individuals who have continued to fan the flames.

Keywords: distinguished level foreign language, history of Level-4 movement, Coalition of Distinguished Language Centers, Journal for Distinguished Language Centers

INTRODUCTION

This article is not meant as a research piece about the "Level 4 Movement"[1] but rather a semi-formal attempt to put into writing an existing oral history before the roots and saplings of previous efforts disappear. To wit, I sorely miss input from the late Boris Shekhtman, who pioneered efforts to formalize and normalize leading learners to achieve near-native levels of proficiency, or, using the Interagency Language Roundtable (ILR) scale (ILR, 2020), to ILR Level 4/4+. I also miss the late Dr. Madeline Ehrman, who accomplished much of the theory and research that accompanied Boris's teaching experience.

THEN

The Origins of Teaching to Level 4

I had just joined the Foreign Service Institute (FSI) in December 1983 as Boris's immediate supervisor, when he and a colleague, Natalia (Natasha) Lord, broached the idea of expanding FSI Russian Department programming beyond the then-current courses that topped out at ILR-3. Jack Mendelsohn, Dean of the School of Language Studies, approved the course and dubbed it the "New Soviet Man" course. I am not sure what motivated him to propose that name, but outside the Russian Department, it stuck. Within the Russian Department, it was known less flamboyantly as the Advanced Course. Students called it the 50-50 course because it offered students a choice of 50 topics and 50 learning tools (methods, techniques, activity types) as well as playfully, given the era in which it was developed, "The Boris & Natasha Show."

The course, once developed, became well known and respected. It helped that the results always achieved the goal of 4/4 (Reading/Speaking). Boris always contended that no learner who entered the program at ILR-3 failed to test at ILR-4 at the end of the 6-month course,[2] and I certainly do not remember any failures though I do remember one ILR-4+ result in reading and speaking, the two skills tested by the FSI.

The content and results of the course were shared widely at the time, and descriptions of the course have appeared in the second language (L2) literature over the years (Leaver & Campbell, 2016; Shekhtman et al., 2002.) Some of the more

---

1   Some research has been done on the topic, most of it mentioned in this article. However, the research is minimal and does not form a large enough body of investigation—yet—to merit an in-depth discussion of the scope and significance. Especially minimal has been the conduct of quantitative research on teaching methods and program design for high-level programs.

2   Unfortunately, records are past the point of being archived and are now in the "lost" category except for incomplete accounts that Boris, perhaps a few others who are now retired, and I have kept in our personal professional files; they are, however, not considered "official" government files. Through the Freedom of Information Act, many US government documents can be obtained, but test records were never archived by the FSI as protected from sharing by the Privacy Act of 1974 (US Code 5, para 552a).

unique aspects of the course that are now becoming standard fare in higher-level-proficiency courses included:

- content-based instruction (Leaver & Bilstein, 2000; Snow & Brinton, 2017;[3] Stryker & Leaver, 1997);
- learner-led curriculum design, a clear precursor of what is today known as Open Architecture Curricular Design (Campbell, 2021; Leaver, 1989);
- emphasis on native speakers' communicative focus in teaching communication skills (Shekhtman & Kupchanka, 2015);
- attention to learner differences (Ehrman, Leaver, & Oxford, 2003; Leaver, 1997; Leaver, Ehrman, & Shekhtman, 2005; and in ESL, Oxford 1990, 2015); and
- real-life tasks (Leaver & Willis, 2005; Nunan, 2014; Willis, 1996).

That course culminated in a professional conference, with presentations and roundtables on a wide variety of social and political topics, attended by the local Russian-speaking community.[4]

Expansion beyond Government

Following those years, some of these practices were reflected sporadically and separately in programs such as the Russian and Arabic programs at the Specialized Language Training Center (SLTC)[5] in Springfield, Virginia, directed by Boris Shekhtman after his retirement from FSI. Otherwise, the Level 4 front remained quiet until San Diego State University (SDSU) was awarded a significant grant from the National Security Education Program (NSEP) to establish the Center for the Advancement of Distinguished Language Proficiency (ADLP Center). Under the direction of Dr. Claudia Angelelli, Christian Degueldre, and myself, with the assistance of Boris Shekhtman and a Board of Advisors of leading language educators, the ADLP Center stood up as a program of the Language Acquisition Research Center (LARC), directed by Dr. Mary Ann Lyman-Hager. The center aimed to spread Level-4 teaching knowledge through faculty development. The areas of

---

3   This is one of several books on the topic written by Ann Snow and Donna Brinton between 1990 and 2020.

4   Examples of materials and approach used in this course to achieve Level 4 (as well as lower levels) can be found in Shekhtman's later works (2003a, 2003b, 2016).

5   The SLTC taught private students, some FSI students who were having difficulty achieving Level 3, and many newspaper reporters, in particular those working at The New York Times and assigned to Moscow. Two of them, Sam Roberts (2017) and Jennifer Krauss (2017), wrote lavish obituaries, lauding Shekhtman's ability to bring students to very high levels of proficiency, which they felt helped them significantly in their work.

specialization of individuals associated with the center were bilingualism, translation, research, language teaching, and language teacher education.[6]

Building the Base: A Coalition of Level 4 Leaders

Shortly after the establishment of the ADLP Center at SDSU, individuals associated with the grant proposal for that organization and with the state of Level 4 language learning and teaching sought to encourage the further sharing of theory, research, and practices. Thus, the Coalition of Distinguished Language Centers (CDLC) was founded, with two physical centers. The primary "headquarters" was located at the SLTC location in Virginia, and a small branch for instruction (as well as, initially, conference support) was established at Howard University in Washington, D.C..

The Components of the Organization

In addition to the ADLP Center, SLTC, and Howard University, the CDLC grew to include several affiliates: the Center for Applied Linguistics (CAL); FSI, Institute für Anglistik/Romanistik, Fachbereich Sprach-und Literaturwissenschaften (University of Kassel, Germany); Jordan Consortium for distinguished-level language studies;[7] ILR; and the Monterey Institute of International Studies (MIIS).[8] Each of these organizations appointed a liaison to the Board of Advisors.

Members of the Board[9] reflected organizations working at the ILR-4 level, whether teaching courses, conducting research, preparing materials, developing theory, or using high-level language (e.g., for interpretation and translation). Members of the Board, chaired by Christian Degueldre (SDSU), included institutional representatives/liaisons and members at large. The latter group were individuals working in the area of very advanced levels of proficiency. The CDLC literature lists the following Board members: Peter Abboud (University of Texas at Austin), Mahdi Alosh (Ohio State University), Claudia Angelelli (SDSU), James Bernhardt (FSI), Ray Clifford (Brigham Young University), Dan E. Davidson (American Councils for International Education [American Councils]), Donald Fischer (University of New Mexico), Nina Garrett (Yale University), Jiaying Howard (MIIS), Deborah Kennedy (CAL), Cornelius Kubler (Williams College), Gerald Lampe (National Foreign Language Center [NFLC]), Betty Lou Leaver (New York Institute of Tech-

---

[6] More information about the early days of the ADLP Center can be found in Lyman-Hager and Degueldre (2004).

[7] The Jordan Consortium included the University of Jordan, Yarmouk University, Jordan University of Science and Technology, and

[8] Today, the MIIS has been renamed the Middlebury Institute of International Studies at Monterey and has become a campus of Middlebury College in Vermont.

[9] These individuals are listed by name because of their personal contributions to the teaching of high levels of language proficiency.

nology [NYIT] in Jordan),[10] Frederic Jackson (ILR), Dr. Maria Lekic (University of Maryland), Boris Shekhtman (SLTC),[11] Kenneth Sheppard (NFLC), Tara Sonenshine (US Institute for Peace), Stephen Stryker (California State University at Stanislaus), Nelleke Van Deusen-Scholl (Yale University), and Mahmud Wardat (Yarmouk University, Jordan).

CDLC Conferences

Although most conferences were conducted annually, in some years the CDLC organized a spring and fall conference. In 2003, the spring conference took place at MIIS in Monterey, California, and the fall conference took place at Howard University. Subsequent conferences took place at the American Councils for International Education, the Maritime Conference Center of the Maritime Institute of Technology and Graduate Studies in Linthicum (Maryland), Carnegie Endowment for International Peace [Carnegie Endowment], and at various hotel conference centers in the Washington, DC area.

Among the keynote speakers were Dr. Richard Brecht (NFLC), Ambassador James Collins (Carnegie Endowment), Dr. Dan E. Davidson (American Councils), Ambassador Ruth Davis (US Department of State), Dr. Donald C. Fischer, Jr. (Defense Language Institute), Dr. Betty Lou Leaver (NYIT), Captain Michael Lopez-Alegria (US Navy and NASA), HRH Prince Firas bin Raad (World Bank and royal family of Jordan), and Tara Sonenshine (US Institute for Peace).

All the conferences were multilingual, with presentations being made in a wide variety of languages: Arabic, Chinese, English, French, German, Russian, and Spanish. The keynote presentation at the first conference in 2003 uniquely manifested the multilingual nature of the conference. Astronaut Michael Lopez-Alegria (2004) delivered the keynote in Spanish in the translation hall at MIIS where students of English, French, Russian, and Spanish in the School of Translation and Interpretation provided formal interpretation into "their" language and attendees dialed into the language desired. After the formal part of his presentation, CAPT (USN) Lopez-Alegria answered questions,[12] responding in one of these four languages, depending upon the language used by the poser of the question, with interpretation continuing in the four languages. It was a tour de force of the linguistic abilities of CAPT Lopez-Alegria and the technological capabilities of the MIIS.

---

10   Betty Lou Leaver also served as Executive Director of the CDLC.

11   Boris Shekhtman also served as Operations Director of the CDLC.

12   The keynote speeches from the first six conferences were published in the conference proceedings: bin Raad (2005), Brecht (2008), Davis (2005), Leaver (2008), Lopez-Alegria (2004), and Sonenshine (2004).

Friend of Distinguished Language Proficiency Award

The CDLC presented an annual "Friend of Distinguished Language Proficiency" for a significant contribution related to studies about the ILR-4 level.[13] A list of recipients of the award is on the masthead of this journal.[14]

CDLC Publications

The CDLC published conference proceedings from the 2003-2006 conferences (Butler & Zhou, 2008; Dubinsky & Butler, 2005; Dubinsky & Robin, 2005; Leaver & Shekhtman, 2004). The conference proceedings included presentations written up as articles as well as collections of slide presentations from the conference. Some of the volumes also included welcoming remarks, conference pictures, and award presentation comments. Most included conference programs and the cumulative list of the individuals who had been presented the Friend of Distinguished Language Proficiency Award. The contributions to the proceedings were published in the language in which they were delivered at the conference, without translation. These volumes are out of print but still available from MSI Press LLC. (www.MSI-Press.com)

A second periodic publication of the CDLC was the Journal for Distinguished Language Studies (JDLS), edited, in turn, by Betty Lou Leaver (2003-2005), Anna Jacobson (2006, 2009-2010), and Boris Shekhtman (2007-2008).[15] The JDLS was published annually from 2003-2010, resulting in 6 volumes. Volume 5 spanned the years 2007 and 2008; Volume 6 spanned the years 2009 and 2010. The journal reflected the same topics as the conferences—theory, research, practice, and personal experience—but did not repeat any of the content. Volume 5 was a special issue and reprinted materials for teaching high levels of Russian proficiency that had been funded by the Department of Education (DOE). The journal accepted articles in world languages from experts in a range of countries. Abstracts in Arabic, Chinese, English, French, German, Russian, and Spanish made information about article contents accessible worldwide. Finally, each issue included a list of recent publications about highly advanced language learning. These early journals are now out of print but still available through MSI Press LLC. Beginning with the current issue, which revives the JDLS and spans the gap years of 2011-2020, articles must be

---

13 A fun fact: Medallion Trophy Shop in Amman, Jordan made all the plaques and, for many years, had a copy of the award presented to HRH Firas bin Raad hanging on its wall.

14 Beginning in 2021, the JDLS editorial board will take on the responsibility of selecting annual recipients of this award. Information about how to nominate someone for the award is available at the publisher's website: https://msipress.com/journal-for-distinguished-language-studies/.

15 The following individuals served as an editorial board for the JDLS: Rajai Rasheed Al-Khanji (University of Jordan), Claudia Angelelli (SDSU), Christian Degueldre (SDSU), Madeline Ehrman (FSI), Surendra Gambhir (University of Pennsylvania), Amal Jaser (Jordan University of Science and Technology), Cornelius Kubler (Williams College), Maria Lekic (University of Maryland), and Rebecca Oxford (University of Maryland).

written in English. However, abstracts of the articles will continue to be included in multiple languages for ease in indexing the articles and journal internationally.

Prior to 2006, the CDLC supported the publication of five books, emanating from CLDC conference presentations and focused on specific practices found to lead learners to higher levels of proficiency. These included Achieving Native-Like Second Language Proficiency: A Catalogue of Critical Factors: Volume 1: Speaking (Leaver, 2003a),[16] Diagnostic Assessment (Cohen, 2004), How to Improve Your Foreign Language Immediately (Shekhtman, 2003a), Individualized Lesson Plans for Very Advanced Foreign Language Students (Leaver, 2003b), and Working with Advanced Foreign Language Students (Shekhtman, 2003b). [17]

In 2006, the CDLC published a collection of teaching techniques proven to work in the classroom and extramurally to get learners to the ILR-4 level: What Works: Helping Students Reach Native-like Second Language Competence. The CDLC served as editor; the collaborative group of authors included Rajai Rasheed Al-Khanji (University of Jordan), James Bernhardt (FSI), Gerd Brendel (Defense Language Institute-Foreign Language Center [DLIFLC]), Tseng Tseng Chang (DLIFLC), Dan Davidson (American Councils), Christian Degueldre (SDSU), Madeline Ehrman (FSI), Surendra Gambhir (University of Pennsylvania), Jiaying Howard (MIIS), Frederick Jackson (ILR), Cornelius Kubler (Williams College), Betty Lou Leaver (CDCL), Maria Lekic (University of Maryland), Natalia Lord (FSI and Howard University), Michael Morrissey (University of Kassel), Boris Shekhtman (SLTC), Kenneth Shepard (NFLC), and Svetlana Sibrina (SLTC). The nature of this little book, known throughout government and academia as "the yellow book" because of its yellow cover,[18] was the presentation of "recipes" 1-2 pages in length, giving the teacher or learner one action to take, generally repetitively, to get closer to the ILR-4 proficiency level.

Materials

In addition to the book publications, the CDLC served as a sharing point for teachers. Wanting to expand the capacity to teach to Level 4, the CDLC encouraged proposals for research and spent much time mentoring junior faculty and providing a form for the presentation of research. As a result, an eclectic combina-

---

16 This book was to be the first of a planned series of four books. Without the support of CDLC, the remaining three volumes were not produced. However, MSI Press has been in touch with the lead author of Achieving Native-Like Second Language Proficiency: A Catalogue of Critical Factors: Volume 2: Writing and plans call for release of this volume in 2021-2022, with the possibility of the remaining two volumes being published in the year(s) following.

17 A second edition of each of these books is planned for release in 2021.

18 When the second edition was published with a grey cover, many users continued to call it the yellow book. The third edition of this book, edited by Thomas Garza (University of Texas at Austin), is due out in late Spring 2021; it will have a yellow cover.

tion of sharable materials was developed. These materials were shown in practice and shared through the annual conferences and the CDLC website.

Feeling a need for more structured sharing, the CDLC turned to the DOE for financial assistance through its materials development grant program and received a grant for the development of Level 4 materials in Russian to be shared with the language community. The goal was to produce generic templates for teaching at higher levels that could be adapted and used for any language as well as full Level-4 courses/seminars in Russian that could be shared at the CDLC website, free for downloading.[19] The templates and materials included three workbooks and a teacher guide. The Russian materials have been used with US government Level-4 learners with good results, based on proficiency scores and formal learner feedback, [20] and a substantial portion of the materials were published in the 2007-2008 special edition of the JDLS.

Finally, with the help of Frederick Jackson, coordinator of the ILR, CDLC maintained an up-to-date annotated bibliography of all books written about Level 4 proficiency. For years, that list was available online for downloading. Unfortunately, that list did not survive the closure of the CDLC in 2010.

More Contributors and More Contributions

ALDP Center Workshops

In the summer of 2002 and 2003, the ADLP Center, supported by NSEP funding and institutional hosting by SDSU, offered workshops on teaching to Level 4 proficiency. These workshops reflected the primary goal of the NSEP grant: to create a large base of teachers able to help learners move from Level 3 to Level 4.

From personal experience as teachers and supervisors, the ADLP Center staff and invited lecturers conducting the workshops were acutely aware of the crippling nature of two myths that had resulted in a dearth of qualified and experienced Level-4 teachers: (1) an assumption that learners cannot be taught successfully at higher levels because learners can and should learn on their own after reaching professional proficiency (ILR 3), and (2) higher level students are easier to teach because they already know how to learn a language. Myths tend to appear logical; facts can often be counterintuitive. This is the case for both of these myths.

---

19 Although the CDLC no longer exists, its website and some of the associated materials and documents were cached at an archive site, https://www.distinguishedlanguagecenters.org. The Russian materials can also be requested as pdf files through MSI Press LLC, the publisher of JDLS.

20 While individual student records maintained at department level within US government language programs are not encapsulated in an institute-wide data based or available in any form that can be shared by the public, Leaver and Campbell (2015) provide some of this data.

Myth 1

The research on learning to Level 4 shows that gaining higher levels of proficiency is not an intuitive process that happens simply by embedding learners with modest language proficiency into foreign situations and hoping that the ensuing set of disorienting dilemmas[21] will push proficiency forward to nativelike speech. With enough time, it generally can do that although there are cases of fossilized Level 2 proficiency among immigrants who have been in country many years. The ability of disorienting dilemmas to shift understanding, recognition, and acceptance of the other is critical to developing higher levels of proficiency and has been found to be an effective producer of high-level language acquisition, but it comes at a price of time. A teacher who recognize and even predicts disorienting dilemmas and serves as a bicultural reference can "hurry along" a more rapid acquisition of nativelike proficiency (Farraj, 2021).

Teachers who have successfully helped learners to reach Level-4 proficiency have anecdotally noticed a significant role for instruction, and learners have reported their perceived need for instruction in a research study conducted by Atwell and Leaver (2002) with the assistance of the Research and Testing Division of the DLIFLC. In this study, learners stated that they had difficulty unraveling some of the more alien aspects of the language and culture they had chosen to learn based on a mere Level-3 language competence that does not include recognizing subtleties not present in their own culture.[22] Among the Level-4 language users who responded to the survey, 75% had found having instruction at the upper levels to be an advantage. In fact, the study showed that instruction at Levels 3-3+ reduced the time to reach Level 4 by as much as 12 years. One reason for the efficacy of instruction at Level 4 is the opportunity to de-fossilize bad habits that grow and become inculcated as learners progress in proficiency. Ehrman (2002) identifies five types of fossilization that have become hold learners at Level 3, often proceeding from the fear of leaving that comfort zone of ease in using the language in order to develop the greater cultural refinements and nuances in language use associated with Level 4. Ehrman labeled these areas of fossilization as

functional (habitually using a restricted vocabulary set, grammar, and syntactic structure);

instruction-fostered (dependence upon a teacher);

domain (restricted number of topical areas);

affective (emotional reactions and affective filters); and

strategic (using a narrow set of learning strategies).

---

21 A disorienting dilemma occurs when a learner comes into contact with a cultural situation (including linguistic behavior) that they cannot understand without changing their perspective, called a transformation by Mezirow (1990), who also coined the term, disorienting dilemma.

22 This would include lexica and structures with illocutionary force, irony, references to literary knowledge and historic experiences shared by native speakers and used implicitly or indirectly in routine discourse and implied social norms.

Successful defossilization generally results in rapid gains in language acquisition but is often dependent upon a knowledgeable instructor in upper-level language learning.

Despite this super-charging of proficiency—gains that learners and teachers found to be a benefit of direct instruction at high levels of proficiency—the development of intercultural competence appears to be dependent to a large extent on in-country experience. Davidson, Garas, and Lekic (2021) demonstrate the quantum gains made during capstone long-term study abroad experiences.[23] The 50-50 course at the FSI required at least three years of living and working abroad, in addition to Level 3 proficiency, for enrollment into the course, intuitively and experientially understanding the reality that Davidson et al. showed empirically two decades later in their study of cultural gains from study abroad programs.

At the 2003 CDCL Fall conference, Shekhtman, Leaver, and Ehrman (2004) answered questions typically asked by students in Level 4 courses. In response to students' question as to the most effective way of reaching Level 4 proficiency, they pointed out that while time spent working, living, and/or studying in country is generally essential (an anticipated response to be sure), classroom time with a knowledgeable teacher-leader after having reached Level 3 proficiency could significantly reduce the time needed to reach nativelike language use and culturally appropriate behavior.

Myth 2

In the 50-50 course at FSI, teachers who at first lined up eagerly to be on the teaching team quickly found out that teaching at this level is not easier than teaching at lower levels. Quite the contrary. Very capable learners tend to be demanding, assuming that they know how they learn best and expecting teachers to adapt and to accede to their demands.[24] The course was called the "Boris and Natasha show" because ultimately other instructors found the challenge of working with very advanced learners too daunting. Thus, what looked to be a wealth of teacher resources turned into a paucity of teachers, reflecting the dearth of Level-4 teachers everywhere.

---

23 These programs had strong academic components, including enrollment of US students in the same courses that native-language students were studying (Davidson, 2015). Similarly, direct enrollment or its equivalent was a staple of the overseas experience of DLIFLC learners who achieved Level 4 in one or more skills.

24 Most teaching approaches do not allow for such extensive flexibility, but Open Architecture Curriculum Design (OACD) (Campbell, 2021) and transformative education (TE) approaches (Leaver, Davidson, and Campbell, 2021) do, and the roots of OACD, which informs TE in language programs, can be traced to the 50-50 course.

Myth Management

The ADLP took on these two myths by conducting a faculty development workshop during the Summer of 2002 and the Summer of 2003. These workshops focused on a deep understanding of Distinguished Language Proficiency with a multi-day presentation and practice session conducted by Sabine Atwell, director of the testing unit at the DLIFLC, and Elvira Swender, training director at the American Council on Teaching Foreign Languages (ACTFL). The workshop focused on practices that those who had taught at Level 4 had found to be successful, with instructors coming from SDSU, SLTC, and several universities. The intent was to be as inclusive as possible.[25]

ACTFL

For its part, ACTFL encouraged the Level 4 teaching and learning conversation that was taking place around the turn of the century. A well-attended pre-conference workshop on teaching for Level 4 proficiency was held a short time after the SDSU workshop. A number of presentations were also given at the ACTFL Annual Meeting.

After the closure of the CDLC, interest in Level 4 at ACTFL waned. The reasons for the waning cannot be fully pinpointed without research that has not taken place, but one suggestion is that the number of learners capable of or needing this level of instruction is dwarfed by the number of beginning language learners, thereby focusing the attention of language program administrators on the needs of the many and leaving little time for the needs of the few.

NFLC

The NFLC was another organization that explored the development of the highest levels of foreign language proficiency in the latter years of the 20th century and early years of the 21st century. Working meetings were conducted to explore the question of language acquisition at high levels of proficiency as well as the characteristics of Distinguished-level speakers. Experts from across the USA and from other countries gathered for these working meetings. To how high a level of proficiency had these participants been able to propel their learners? One of the Arabic-language participants laid out a reading program with the goal of ILR 4+ (Badawi, 2002), and subsequent to these working meetings, the NFLC established

---

[25] It should be noted that a decade earlier, NEH funded eight summer Institutes in Russian Language and Culture at Bryn Mawr College for teachers to improve their own language proficiency; these institutes were conducted in Russian by the Center of Russian Language and Culture at Friends School (CORLAC) in Baltimore (MD), supported by the American Council for Teachers of Russian (ACTR), and reported on in Dabars and Kagan (2002).

reading programs in Chinese, English, Hindi, and Spanish, with a goal of Level 4 proficiency (Ingold, 2002).

From these meetings came a number of new understandings—or at least, refined understandings—of concepts associated with Level 4 proficiency. Many of the early Level-4 articles and book chapters were written by those who had participated in the NLFC working meetings.

In addition to these published pieces, a manual for those teaching to Level 4 was prepared by Madeline Ehrman and Betty Lou Leaver, who were then part-time associates at the NFLC. The manual focused on formative assessment, identifying "cusp levels," or specific lexical, grammatical, sociolinguistic, discourse, fluency, and other features that needed to be acquired to move from 3+ to 4 proficiency.[26] While the manual was never formally published but rather passed around among government language programs (which meant that it has disappeared over time), the knowledge remains, thanks to laminated cusp charts still in use at least by some diagnostic assessors conducting formative assessments at the DLIFLC.[27]

The Language Flagship

Soon after the ADLP Center and the CDLC were established,[28] the National Security Education Program (NSEP) funded flagship programs at a number of institutions (Murphy & Evans-Romaine, 2016). Today, the flagships number 31 programs at 21 institutions (The Language Flagship, 2021).[29] Flagships posit three goals: (1) professional-level language proficiency (ILR 3); (2) advanced cultural skills, coming from experience in living and working in host-language countries: and (3) development of intercultural insights to inform future language careers.

While the proficiency goal of the Language Flagship program is Level 3 proficiency, many learners have reached Level 4, especially in the Russian flagships, where faculty have arguably more experience at working at this level than do faculty in other languages. Davidson (2015), for example, provides statistics that show post-program results as high as ILR 4 for participants in its study abroad components of Russian language programs. The Iron Curtain that segregated East from West during the Cold War may have contributed to a greater experience of Russian teachers at the higher levels of experience since it forced learners to achieve high levels of proficiency in the classroom, whereas learners of world languages like French, Spanish, Italian, Portuguese, etc., had opportunities for study abroad where

---

26 The manual was later expanded to include cusps for all proficiency levels. (Updating and more research both on content and application

27 From 2006 through 2017, the Continuing Education Division at the DLIFLC maintained a Diagnostic Assessment Center devoted to training teachers how to conduct formative assessments and how to coach learners in the application of the results.

28 The flagships date from 2002, but their actual funding and stand-up came near the end of the year, whereas the ADLP was stood up in January of that year.

29 The Language Flagship website gives conflicting numbers: 23 institutions vs. 21 institutions.

many of them achieved their higher levels of proficiency. As a result, teachers of Russian were pushed to find ways to accommodate higher levels of learning in the classroom and, in some cases, emulate the host country environment.

A Study of Jordanian Students

In 2005, researchers at the University of Jordan, Jordan University of Science and Technology, and the Jordan campus of NYIT collaborated on a project to identify demographics that might be associated with those native speakers of Arabic who ultimately achieved near-native proficiency in English writing. Funded by the Conference on College Composition and Communication (CCCC) of the National Council of Teachers of English, the collaborators tested 65 students, evenly split between male and female genders and roughly ages 18-22, thought to be at near-native levels of foreign language proficiency. However, only 21 participants tested at this level, with the others testing strongly at Level 3/3+ proficiency. The advantage to the split was the ability to compare the demographics of both groups, with the unexpected finding that all Level 4 writers had experienced a bilingual or multilingual childhood (even though some never learned any of the languages in their neighborhood). The disadvantage to the split is that the resulting Level 4 population was a very small sample size, and another, larger sampling will be needed for confirmation of the findings. [30]

Findings from this study have been shared in several venues. These include presentations at the CCCC and other conferences, sharing with home universities, and publications, including in the JDLS (e.g., Jaser et al., 2005).

DLIFLC

From 2006-2017,[31] the DLIFLC experienced increasing success at delivering graduates of its intermediate and advanced courses at Level 4 proficiency in one or more skills, including one graduate of the Defense Threat Reduction Agency (DTRA) intermediate specialty course,[32] who achieved Level 4 across all tested skills: listening, reading, speaking.[33] A major component of these courses was a short study period, averaging four weeks, in country, where students were enrolled

---

30 Finding an adequate sample size may not be possible, given the relatively low number of high-level speakers/writers in any language (e.g., State Department, which trains large numbers of diplomats in Russian estimates only 160 of those trained of the years have achieved a Level 4—based on my access to FSI records while I was working there and later at other US government language schools).

31 In 2018, the intermediate and advanced course instructors were blended into the basic course programs, and the emphasis on achieving ILR 4 has disappeared, based on changing (lowered) requirements for DLIFLC graduates, dating from that time.

32 Intermediate courses generally lasted 37 weeks, but the DTRA course was ten weeks longer to allow time to learn the content and language of the US-Russia treaties associated with their future duties.

33 Writing is not tested at DLIFCL although the intermediate and advanced courses did teach it. The presumption was that the writing skill level would most likely match the speaking skill level. However, without testing there was no evidence for that widely held belief.

in regular university classes with their host-country peers or received the equivalent instruction in content courses taught by professors using lecture materials from their regular courses. Professional-level activities in the community were planned for each day to facilitate interactive speaking skills. (In countries like Jordan and Morocco, an additional hour was added each day to work with a language teacher on acquiring the local dialect of Arabic.) These courses are described in detail in Campbell (2021), Farraj (2021), and Leaver and Campbell (2015, 2020).

Government Associations

Interest flagged at universities in the years that followed. However, two government organizations have kept the Level 4 movement alive through their interest in testing the highest levels of proficiency.

The Interagency Language Roundtable, whose monthly meetings draw 75-100 participants from the US government, academia, and private industry, have devoted a component of the roundtable to the development of standards for language, and more recently, for culture. Occasional meetings focus on how to test for Level ILR 4.[34]

The Bureau of International Language Coordination (BILC), subordinate to the North Atlantic Treaty Organization (NATO), has worked on developing definitions of Level 4 through its Standardized Agreements (STANAG). BILC, whose responsibility it is to keep NATO nations informed of advances in foreign language training, convenes an annual conference and an annual professional seminar, attended by representatives from member nations.[35] STANAG 6001 establishes proficiency level descriptions, including for Level 4.

Models and Materials

In the early days, CDLC institutions wishing to implement Distinguished-level proficiency programs not only suffered from a lack of experience but also from a lack of models.[36] The annual CDLC conferences served a worthy purpose of bringing together experienced teachers and administrators with those seeking to establish programs/courses. In this way, the CDLC conferences provided a platform for showcasing programs, results, and materials.

Among those producing materials in the early days of the Level 4 Movement was the American Council of Teachers of Russian (ACTR). These online materials reflected authentic language, authentically produced texts, and self-study lessons that could also be used in courses (Leaver, Ehrman, & Lekic, 2004).

---

[34] More information about the ILR can be found at its website, https://www.govtilr.org/IRL%20History.htm#.

[35] More information about BILC can be found at its website: https://www.natobilc.org/en/.

[36] The 50/50 course was designed nearly exclusively on the basis of faculty personal experience and successful learners' contributions and suggestions.

Another of set contributors to the collection of high-level teaching materials were faculty at the Center for Language Study at Yale. Their specific contributions featured high-level cultural studies in the target language (Tortora & Crocetti, 2005; van Altena, 2008).

As noted earlier, the CDLC annual conferences facilitated the sharing of materials development and the distribution of developed materials from various universities and US government language programs. Among these were high-level materials in Chinese, developed by Cornelius Kubler (2004) at Williams College, and materials for a course in business Spanish taught by Roberta Lavine (2004) at the University of Maryland.

Another way in which the CDLC annual conferences provided a service to the Distinguished-level teaching and learning community was the sharing of program models, These models included relatively mature programs, like the NEH-CORLAC summer Russian Language Institutes at Bryn Mawr College (Dabars & Kagan, 2002; Jackson, 2004), and newly emerging programs, like the Language Flagships (Lekic & Shakhova, 2005; Ryding & Bergman, 2005). Presentations by program directors not only described programs but shared insights into successes and challenges.

Publications

In addition to the publications mentioned above, a small but important collection of books and articles put into print newly emerging research, theory, and applications for teaching to Level 4 proficiency. With the exception of one volume that focused primarily on Level 3 but made some references to Level 4, emanating from a 2013 conference at Brigham Young University (Brown & Bown, 2015), most of these publications came into print between 2002 and 2010.

In 2001, the ACTR Letter, a quarterly publication, started publishing short articles about Level-4 concepts in its "Front Page Dialogue."[37] Those articles were republished in full in Twelve Years of Teaching Russian (Leaver, 1999) and partially in the Journal for Distinguished Language Studies (Brecht et al., 2005).

Prior to the establishing of the CDLC, two books helped immensely with prompting a Level 4 movement: Content-Based Instruction in Foreign Language Education (Stryker & Leaver, 1997) and Languages across the Curriculum (Kecht & von Hammerstein, 2000). These two books were very helpful in providing the models and sample programs for structuring Level 4 study.

---

37 The "Front Page Dialogue" (FPD), which was added to the ACTR Letter in 1987, was a short piece, often argumentative, that began on the first page of the newsletter of a topic that was followed from 1-3 years. Russian teachers and professors "argued" with each through subsequent "dialogues." When all opinions had been exhausted, a new topic was chosen. The FPD has been a popular feature of the ACTR Letter and continues in popularity as of the writing of this article, 33 years later.

However, the seminal work, the book that started it all, was Developing Professional-Level Second Language Instruction (Leaver & Shekhtman, 2002). That book, besides identifying underlying concepts unique to upper-level language study and programs (Byrnes, 2002; Leaver & Shekhtman, 2002), described eight differing, significant, and successful Level 4 programs (e.g., Angelelli & Degueldre, 2002: Kubler, 2002; Dabars & Kagan, 2002) and, in so doing, built excitement around the growing conviction that learners can achieve near-native levels even in the absence of study abroad. What they mostly cannot do is to go it alone; they need teachers to "spell out" the things that they cannot see, those 4/4+ nuances that are so culturally biased that no foreigner would figure them out without the help of a series of disorienting dilemmas (which can take much longer than the work of a teacher in a classroom), or a highly educated bicultural and bilingual native speaker, as confirmed by Leaver and Atwell (2002) in the study cited above.

About the same time, some academics involved with high-level teaching and learning published results of their observations and findings, mostly in a handful of books, edited or co-authored by Dr. Heidi Byrnes of Georgetown University (Byrnes, 2007; Byrnes & Maxim, Eds., 2003; Byrnes, Weger-Guntharp, & Spring, 2006; Ortega & Byrnes, 2008).[38] These books expanded the Level-4 discussion in important ways.

While most of the CDLC and other Level 4 publications have focused on the paths taken, materials needed, and programs designed to achieve Level 4, some researchers in intersecting fields have also displayed an interest in Level 4 e.g., summative and formative testing (Cohen, 2003; Fischer, 2004), programs and issues in translation and interpretation (Angelelli & Degueldre, 2002), and issues related to heritage learning programs, some of which promote goals of near-native language acquisition (Angelelli & Kagan, 2002).

AND NOW

With the passage of time, expertise has been lost as members of the CDLC and individuals working at the Distinguished level of proficiency at that time have moved on[39] or, unfortunately, died.[40] As a result, the practices that took the students of the earlier practitioners to Level 4 have, to a large extent, disappeared.

Fortuitously, two highly respected publishers stand out in their support of publications promoting Distinguished Level Proficiency: Cambridge University Press and Georgetown University Press. The majority of serious work published and widely distributed on the topic on a world-wide basis, as well as seminal work in

---

38 Dr. Byrnes was a significant contributor to the Leaver and Shekhtman (2002) seminal work on developing professional level language proficiency.

39 A large number of the original CDLC members, including most of its founders, have retired.

40 Among the most significant among the deceased are Dr. Madeline Ehrman and Boris Shekhtman, both of whom made immense contributions to the Level 4 Movement while alive..

the Level-4 area, have come from these two academic publishers. They have not backed off from taking on futuristic projects that move into reality and then into popularity. With a renewed interest in achieving Level 4 proficiency—if it comes, as a number of us hope it will—other publishers might well consider jumping on the bandwagon.

The financial support of the NSEP and the DOE made the inroads into developing and disseminating Level 4 programs possible. While the CDLC provided the strongest impetus and the mechanics for pulling together academics and practitioners, a significant tool of the CDLC was The Journal for Distinguished Language Studies (JDLS). After a period of dormancy, it is exciting to see its re-emergence in 2020, thanks to individuals associated with CDLC's earlier activities and some newcomers to the Level 4 movement, who have stepped up to serve as editors and advisors.[41] The hope and goal are that the JDLS will now serve as a stride forward into a new era of renewed interest in Level 4 research, teaching, learning, and testing and revised, brave program goals that expect to produce language professionals capable of functioning as closely as possible to their native-language partners in using language for the common good,[42] among its many roles.

References

Angelelli, C., & Degueldre, C. (2002). Bridging the gap between language for general purposes and language for work: an intensive Superior-level language/skill course for teachers, translators, and interpreters. In B. L. Leaver & B. Shekhtman (Eds.). *Developing professional-level foreign language proficiency* (pp. 61-76). Cambridge, UK: Cambridge University Press.

Angelelli, C. & Kagan, O. (2002). Heritage speakers as learners at the Superior level: differences and similarities between Spanish and Russian student populations. In B. L. Leaver & B. Shekhtman (Eds.). *Developing professional-level foreign language proficiency* (pp. 197-218). Cambridge, UK: Cambridge University Press.

Badawi, E. (2002). In the quest for the Level 4+ in Arabic: Training Level 2-3 learners in independent reading. In B. L. Leaver & B. Shekhtman (Eds.). *Developing professional-level foreign language proficiency* (pp. 156-176). Cambridge, UK: Cambridge University Press.

Bernhardt, J. E, Campbell, C. M., & Leaver, B. L. (2020). Can foreign languages be taught for peace at US government institutes? In R. L. Oxford, M. M. Oliver, M. Harrison, T. Gregerson, Eds., *Peacebuilding in language education: Innovations in theory and practice* (pp. 129-145). Bristol, UK: Multilingual Matters.

---

41 The advisory board is listed on the masthead.

42 It might be pertinent to point out that there is a growing recognition of the role that high levels of language skills and intercultural competence can play not only in traditional activities but also for building international peace (Bernhardt, Campbell, & Leaver, 2020; Oxford et al,, 2020).

bin Raad, HRH Firas. (2005). Keynote speech. In I. Dubinsky & D. B. Butler, Eds., *Teaching and learning to near-native levels of language proficiency III: Proceedings of the Fall 2005 annual conference of the Coalition of Distinguished Language Centers* (pp. 9-14). Salinas, CA: MSI Press.

Brecht, R. D. (2008). Keynote speech. In D. B. Butler & Y. Zhou, Y., Eds. (2008). *Teaching and learning to near-native levels of proficiency IV: Proceedings of the Spring & Fall 2006 conferences of the Coalition of Distinguished Language Centers* (pp. 85-90). San Juan Bautista, CA: MSI Press.

Brecht, R.D., Leaver, B. L., Lekic, M. D., & Shekhtman, B. (2005). Essays about high-level language learning and teaching: Reprints from the *ACTR Letter. Journal for Distinguished Language Studies* 3: 63-78.

Brown, T., & Bown, J., Eds. (2015). *To advanced proficiency and beyond; Theory and methods for developing Superior second language ability*. Washington, DC: Georgetown University Press.

Butler, D. B. & Zhou, Y., Eds. (2008). *Teaching and learning to near-native levels of proficiency IV: Proceedings of the Spring & Fall 2006 conferences of the Coalition of Distinguished Language Centers*. San Juan Bautista, CA: MSI Press.

Byrnes, H. (2007). Advanced language learning: The contribution of Halliday and Vygotsky. NYC: Continuum.

Byrnes, H., & Maxim, H., Eds. (2003). *Advanced foreign language learning*, AAUSC [American Association of University and School Coordinators] volume. Boston: Heinle

Byrnes, H., Weger-Guntharp, H. D., & Sprang, K. A., Eds. (2006). *Educating for Advanced foreign language capacities: Constructs, curriculum, instruction, assessment*. Washington, DC: Georgetown University press.

Campbell, C. (2021). Open Architecture Curricular Design: A Fundamental Principle of Transformative Language Learning and Teaching. In B. L. Leaver, D. Davidson,, & C. Campbell, Eds. *Transformative Language Learning and Teaching* (pp. 43-50). Cambridge, UK: Cambridge University Press.

Coalition of Distinguished Language Centers. (2006). *What works: Helping students reach native-like second-language competence*. Silver Spring, MD: MSI Press.

Cohen, B. (2004). *Diagnostic assessment at the Superior/Distinguished threshold*. Salinas, CA: MSI Press.

Dabars, Z., & Kagan, O. (2002). Teaching Russian language teachers in eight summer Institutes in Russian language and culture. In B. L. Leaver & B. Shekhtman (Eds.). *Developing professional-level foreign language proficiency* (pp. 219-242). Cambridge, UK: Cambridge University Press

Davidson, D. E. (2015). The development of L2 proficiency and literacy within the context of the federally supported overseas language training programs for Americans. In T. Brown & J. Bown, Eds., *To Advanced Proficiency and beyond: Theory and methods for developing Superior second-language ability* (pp. 117-150). Washington, D.C.: Georgetown University Press.

Davidson, D. E., Garas, N., & Lekic, M. D. (2021). Transformative language learning in the overseas immersion environment: Exploring affordances of intercultural development. In B. L. Leaver, D. E. Davidson, & C. Campbell, Eds., *Transformative language learning and teaching* (pp. 109-119). Cambridge, UK: Cambridge University Press.

Davis, R. A. (2005). Keynote address. In I. Dubinsky & R. Robin, Eds., *Teaching and learning to near-native levels of language proficiency II: Proceedings of the Fall 2004 annual conference of the Coalition of Distinguished Language Centers* (pp. 7-12). Salinas, CA: MSI Press.

Dubinsky, I., & Butler, D. B. (2005). *Teaching and learning to near-native levels of proficiency III: Proceedings of the Fall 2005 annual conference of the Coalition of Distinguished Language Centers.* Salinas, CA: MSI Press.

Dubinsky, I., & R. Robin, R. . (2005). *Teaching and learning to near-native levels of proficiency II: Proceedings of the Fall 200 annual conference of the Coalition of Distinguished Language Centers.* San Juan Bautista, CA: MSI Press.

Ehrman, M. E., Leaver, B. L., & Oxford, R. L. (2003). A brief overview of individual differences in second language learning. System 31(3): 313-330.

Farraj, A. (2021). Transformative dimensions of community engagement and service learning during in-country immersion. In B. L. Leaver, D. E. Davidson, & C. Campbell, Eds., *Transformative language learning and teaching* (pp. 120-128). Cambridge, UK: Cambridge University Press.

Fischer, Jr., D. C. (2004). Testing from a distance to learning from a distance to near-native proficiency. In B. L. Leaver & B. Shekhtman, Eds., *Teaching and learning to near-native levels of language proficiency: Proceedings of the Spring and Fall 2003 conferences of the Coalition of Distinguished Language Centers* (pp. 103-112). Salinas, CA: MSI Press.

Ingold, C. (2002). The LangNet "Reading to the Four" project: Applied technology at higher levels of language learning. In B. L. Leaver & B. Shekhtman (Eds.). *Developing professional-level foreign language proficiency* (pp. 141-155). Cambridge, UK: Cambridge University Press.

Interagency Language Roundtable. (2020). Description of proficiency levels. Interagency Language Roundtable Downloaded from https://www.govtilr.org/Skills/ILRscale1.htm.

Jaser, A., Al-Khanji, R. R., & Leaver, B. L. (2005). A demographic analysis of Arabic-speaking students who achieve native-like levels in English-writing skills. *Journal for Distinguished Language Studies* 3: 41-62/.

Kecht, M-R., & con Hammerstein, K. (2000). *Languages across the curriculum: Interdisciplinary structures and internationalized education.* Columbus, OH: Ohio State University Press.

Krauss, J. (2017, April 10). Learning Russian from "Boris Badenov." *The New York Times.* Downloaded January 16, 2021 from https://nytimes.com/insider/learning-Russian-from-Boris-Badenov.html.

Kubler, C. (2002). Learning Chinese in China: Programs for developing Superior-to-Distinguished-level language proficiency in China and Taiwan. In B. L. Leaver & B. Shekhtman (Eds.). *Developing professional-level foreign language proficiency* (pp. 96-118). Cambridge, UK: Cambridge University Press.

Kubler, C. (2004). Preparing materials for high-level learners of Chinese. In B. L. Leaver & B. Shekhtman, Eds., *Teaching and learning to near-native levels of language proficiency: Proceedings of the Spring and Fall 2003 conferences of the Coalition of Distinguished Language Centers* (pp. 127-134). Salinas, CA: MSI Press.

Jackson, F. H. (2004). Observations on training beyond-3 in an institutional setting. In B. L. Leaver & B. Shekhtman, Eds., *Teaching and learning to near-native levels of language proficiency: Proceedings of the Spring and Fall 2003 conferences of the Coalition of Distinguished Language Centers* (pp. 135-140). Salinas, CA: MSI Press.

Lavine, R. (2004). Business Spanish at high levels of proficiency. B. L. Leaver & B. Shekhtman, Eds., *Teaching and learning to near-native levels of language proficiency: Proceedings of the Spring and Fall 2003 conferences of the Coalition of Distinguished Language Centers* (pp. 147-152). Salinas, CA: MSI Press.

Leaver, B. L. (1989, February). Dismantling classroom walls for increased foreign language proficiency. *Foreign Language Annals* 22(1): 67-74.

Leaver, B. L. (1997). *Teaching the whole class.* Thousand Oaks, CA: Corwin Press.

Leaver, B. L., Ed. (1999). *Twelve years of dialogue on teaching Russian: From the Front Pages of the ACTR Letter 1988-1999.* Washington, DC: ACTR/ACCELS Publications.

Leaver, B. L. (2003a). *Achieving native-like second language proficiency: A catalogue of critical factors: Volume 1: Speaking.* Salinas, CA: MSI Press.

Leaver, B. L. (2003b). *Individualized study plans for very advanced students of foreign languages.* Salinas, CA: MSI Press.

Leaver, B. L. (2008). Keynote speech. In D. B. Butler & Y. Zhou, Y., Eds. (2008). Teaching and learning to near-native levels of proficiency IV: Proceedings of the Spring & Fall 2006 conferences of the Coalition of Distinguished Language Centers (pp. 9-14). San Juan Bautista, CA: MSI Press.

Leaver, B. L., & Bilstein, P. (2000). Content, language, and task in content-based programs. In M-R. Kecht & K. von Hammerstein. Languages across the curriculum (pp. 79-118). Columbus, OH: Ohio State University.

Leaver, B. L., & Campbell, C. (2015). Experience with higher levels of proficiency. In T. Brown & J. Bown, Eds. To Advanced proficiency and beyond: Theory and methods for developing superior second language ability (pp. 3-22). Washington, DC: Georgetown University Press.

Leaver, B. L., & Campbell, C. (2020). The shifting paradigm in Russian pedagogy: From Communicative Language Teaching to transformative language learning and teaching. In E. Dengub, I. Dubinina, & J. Merrill, Eds., The art of teaching Russian (pp. 147-152). Washington, DC: Georgetown University Press.

Leaver, B. L., Davidson, D. E., & Campbell, C. (2021). *Transformative language learning and teaching.* Cambridge, UK: Cambridge University Press.

Leaver, B. L., Ehrman, M. E., & Lekic, M. D. (2004, December). Distinguished-level learning online: Support materials from LangNet and RussNet. Foreign Language Annals 37(4):556-565.

Leaver, B. L., Ehrman, M. E., & Shekhtman, B. (2005). *Achieving success in second language acquisition.* Cambridge, UK: Cambridge University Press.

Leaver, B. L. & Shekhtman, B., Eds. (2002) *Developing professional-level foreign language proficiency.* Cambridge, UK: Cambridge University Press.

Leaver, B. L., & Shekhtman, B. (2004). *Teaching and learning to near-native levels of proficiency: Proceedings of the Spring & Fall 2003 conferences of the Coalition of Distinguished Language Centers.* Salinas, CA: MSI Press.

Leaver, B. L., & Willis, J. (2005). *Task-based instruction in foreign language education: Practices and Programs.* Washington, DC: Georgetown University Press.

Lekic, M. D., & Shakhova, D. The Russian Flagship Program: Year one results and year two refinements. In I. Dubinsky & D. B. Butler, Eds., *Teaching and learning to near-native levels of language proficiency III: Proceedings of the Fall 2005 annual conference of the Coalition of Distinguished Language Centers* (pp. 111-122). Salinas, CA: MSI Press.

Lopez-Alegria, M. (2004). Keynote speech. In B. L. Leaver & B. Shekhtman. (2004). *Teaching and learning to near-native levels of proficiency: Proceedings of the Spring & Fall 2003 conferences of the Coalition of Distinguished Language Centers* (pp. 3-12). Salinas, CA: MSI Press.

Lyman-Hager, M. A., & Degueldre, C. (2004). Establishing a center for Level 4 study: Issues and agendas. In B. L. Leaver & B. Shekhtman, eds., *Teaching and learning to near-native levels of language proficiency: Proceedings of the Spring and Fall 2003 conferences of the Coalition of Distinguished Language Centers* (pp. 115-127). Salinas, CA: MSI Press.

Morley, J. (2005). English for Academic Purposes: Trends in oral communication instruction. In I. Dubinsky & R. Robin, Eds., *Teaching and learning to near-native levels of language proficiency II: Proceedings of the 2004 annual conference of the Coalition of Distinguished Language Centers* (pp. 93-100). Salinas, CA: MSI Press.

Murphy, D., & Evans-Romaine, K. (2016). *Exploring the US Language Flagship: Professional competence in a second language by graduation.* Bristol, UK: Multilingual Matters.

Nunan, D. (2004). *Task-based language learning.* Cambridge: Cambridge University Press.

Ortega, L., & Byrnes. H. (2008). *The longitudinal study of advanced L2 capacities.* London: Routledge.

Oxford, R. L. (1990). *Language learning strategies: What every teacher should know.* Boston: Heinle.

Oxford, R. L. (2015). *Teaching and researching: Language learning strategies.* London: Routledge.

Oxford, R. L., Olivero, M. M., Harrison, M., & Gregersen, T., Eds. (2020). *Peacebuilding in language education: Innovations in theory and practice.* Bristol, UK: Multilingual Matters.

Roberts, S. (2017, March 24). Boris V. Shekhtman, who taught Russian to journalists and diplomats, dies at 77. The New York Times. Downloaded January 16, 2021 from https://nytimes.com/2017/03/24/world/boris-v-shekhtman-who-taught-Russian-to-journalists-and-diplomats-dies-at-776.html.

Ryding, K., & Bergman, E. (2005). Arabic Flagship: Issues in curriculum design. In I. Dubinsky & D. B. Butler, Eds., *Teaching and learning to near-native levels of language proficiency III: Proceedings of the Fall 2005 annual conference of the Coalition of Distinguished Language Centers* (pp. 59-64). Salinas, CA: MSI Press.

Shekhtman, B. (2003a). *How to improve your foreign language immediately.* Salinas, CA: MSI Press.

Shekhtman, B. (2003b). *Working with advanced foreign language students.* Salinas, CA: MSI Press.

Shekhtman, B., Ed. (2016). *How to use your Russian in communication effectively.* CreateSpace.

Shekhtman, B., Leaver, B. L., Lord, N. A., Kuznetsova, E., & Ovtcharenko, E. (2002). Developing professional-level oral proficiency: The Shekhtman Method of Communicative Teaching. In B. L. Leaver & B. Shekhtman (Eds.). Developing professional-level foreign language proficiency (pp. 119-140). Cambridge, UK: Cambridge University Press.

Shekhtman, B. & Kupchanka, D. (2015). *Communicative focus: Teaching foreign language on the basis of the native speaker's communicative focus.* Virginia Beach, VA: Villa Magna LLC.

Snow, A., & Brinton, D. (2017). *The content-based classroom, second edition: New perspectives on integrating language and content.* Ann Arbor, MI: University of Michigan Press.

Sonenshine. T. (2004). Keynote speech. In B. L. Leaver & B. Shekhtman, Eds., *Teaching and learning to near-native levels of proficiency: Proceedings of the Spring & Fall 2003 conferences of the Coalition of Distinguished Language Centers* (pp. 13-16). Salinas, CA: MSI Press.

Stryker, S., & Leaver, B. L. (1997). *Content-based instruction in foreign language education: Models and methods.* Washington, DC: Georgetown University Press.

The Language Flagship. (2021). The next generation of language professionals. The Language Flagship. Downloaded January 18, 2021 from https://www.thelanguageflagship.org/.

Tortora, M., & Crocetti, M. (2005). An interdisciplinary approach to Advanced through Distinguished language acquisition: Bridge courses. In I. Dubinsky & D. B. Butler, Eds., *Teaching and learning to near-native levels of language proficiency III: Proceedings of the Fall 2005 annual conference of the Coalition of Distinguished Language Centers* (pp. 59-64). Salinas, CA: MSI Press.

van Altena, A. M. (2008). Fortalecimiento de la precisión léxica y sintáctica en español: actividades conducentes a la reflexión. In D. B. Butler & Y. Zhou, Eds., *Teaching and learning to near-native levels of language proficiency IV: Proceedings of the Spring and Fall 2006 conferences of the Coalition of Distinguished Language Centers* (pp. 179-186). San Juan Bautista, CA: MSI Press.

Willis, J. (1996). *A framework for task-based learning.* London: Pearson Longman.

Rethinking the Rating Process: Solution to the Threshold Performance Dilemma

Mary Jo DiBiase-Lubrano, Yale University (USA)
Jana Vasilj-Begovic, Department of National Defence (CAN)

Abstract

Test reliability and intrinsically, validity are indisputably linked to valid scoring criteria. When assessing constructed responses in very advanced language proficiency level tests specifically, the extent of the raters' level of training and norming to the criteria, and their ability to foresee all possibly correct responses are critical. These issues have a bearing in standard setting methods aiming to establish two meaningful categories of candidates who meet and do not meet the minimum criterial levels of performance, which exemplify the construct and reflect the test purpose. This conceptual paper describes an approach to establishing cut scores in an integrated reading comprehension test via the skill of writing, which purports to measure Distinguished proficiency reading skills via constructed responses. A mixed method approach is adopted in which raters' holistic ratings are triangulated with their analytic scores. The method, which the authors called the Retrodictive Modeling Approach (RMA), relies on raters' level of expertise and holistic ratings coupled with their qualitative analysis and scores, which yield a pattern useful for establishing a threshold performance level. Although claims to generalizability are beyond the scope of this study, further research may lead to a wider use of the RMA in Distinguished proficiency level testing.

Keywords: standard setting; norming; scoring validity, Distinguished levels

Very advanced proficiency testing, such as the Distinguished level on the American Council on the Teaching of Foreign Languages (ACTFL) proficiency guidelines or Level 4 on the Interagency Language Roundtable (ILR) proficiency scale presents unique challenges given the limitations of the test design, the selection of appropriate item tasks, the level of rater training, and the choice of appropriate scoring techniques. Nonetheless, while the usefulness of testing Distinguished or Level 4 proficiency levels is beyond the scope of this study, there are contexts and job descriptions which entail the use of highly articulated and nuanced language. One such context is language proficiency in specific headquarters within the North Atlantic Treaty Alliance (NATO), where military and civilian job descriptions call for STANAG Level 4 proficiency in one or more skills (LNA, 2015). To address the complexities of testing at such high levels, the Bureau of International Language Coordination (BILC), NATO's advisory body for language training and testing matters, was tasked with establishing a working group to develop a prototype of a reading comprehension test at Level 4 according to the proficiency scale in use among NATO countries, the Standardization Agreement No. 6001. Since testing at STANAG 6001 Level 4 was groundbreaking, the working group agreed to start from the skill of reading, because it was considered to be the easiest of the four skills to measure. The purpose of this test was to measure the reading proficiency at STANAG 6001 Level 4, while the use of the test scores would be to certify the reading proficiency of military and civilians whose positions entailed such a high level of literacy. Although testing is considered a national responsibility, BILC assists nations with test development by promoting best practices and by fostering a uniform interpretation of the STANAG 6001 language proficiency descriptors, used as a guideline for curriculum and test development, as well as for the construct of general proficiency. The ultimate goal of BILC's efforts is to contribute to interoperability within NATO's multi-national operations and deployments, contexts in which English is used as the main language of communication, and at the same time, recognized as a significant impediment to interoperability. The STANAG 6001 has been in use since 1976 (Edition 1), and constitutes the underpinning for standardized testing practices and procedures in NATO, Partnership for Peace countries (PfP), and other global partner nations that wish to certify their personnel with linguistic profiles based on this standard. While the document has been updated several times since 1976, the changes only regard the preface and instructions to participating nations, whereas the actual proficiency descriptors have remained unchanged since its 2003 edition.

To carry out this project, BILC formed a working group (WG), selected on members' level of expertise in working with the scale, and their documented background as test developers in their country of residence (Bulgaria, Canada, Denmark, Germany, the Netherlands, Sweden, and the USA). The group was tasked with the development of an advisory/prototype test starting with the skill of reading, defined in STANAG 6001 as the expert level and described as:

"Demonstrates strong competence in reading all styles and forms of the written language used for professional purposes, including texts from unfamiliar general and professional-specialist areas. Contexts include newspapers, magazines, and professional literature written for the well-educated reader and may contain topics from such areas as economics, culture, science, and technology, as well as from the reader's own field. Can readily follow unpredictable turns of thought on any subject matter addressed to the general reader. Shows both global and detailed understanding of texts including highly abstract concepts. Can understand almost all cultural references and can relate a specific text to other written materials within the culture. Demonstrates a firm grasp of stylistic nuances, irony, and humour. Reading speed is similar to that of a native reader. Can read reasonably legible handwriting without difficulty." (STANAG 6001, 2016, A-6).

STANAG 6001 is a criterion-referenced scale in which each descriptor can be considered a separate construct (Clifford, 2013 personal communication) for test development purposes in a particular skill, and for a particular proficiency level. All STANAG 6001 descriptors contain information that relates to the content domains, language tasks, accuracy statements and text types, i.e. length and organization of text. The latter two inform the fundamental rating criteria used in the productive skills, whereas in the receptive skills, the statements serve to describe the nature of the written or audio passages the language user is able to comprehend. Thus, a proficiency level can represent a separate construct which contains all necessary components for test construction such, as domains, language tasks, accuracy, and text length. For Level 4 reading, the breakdown of the descriptor is illustrated below where content refers to the topical domains, as well as sources of higher-level texts; the linguistic tasks are the operations the reader needs to perform in order to process the text, while accuracy defines how well (conditions) the reader can understand the text. The text type, not specifically mentioned in the tri-section, is understood to be of essay length discourse (STANAG 6001, 2016, A-6).

CONTENT

All styles and forms of writing used for professional purposes, including texts from unfamiliar general and professional-specialist areas.

Newspapers, magazines, and professional literature written for well-educated native readers.

Highly abstract concepts.

Reasonably legible handwriting.

TASKS

Follow unpredictable turns of thought on any subject matter addressed to the general reader.
Show both global and detailed understanding of texts.
Understand almost all cultural references.

ACCURACY

Can relate a specific text to other written materials in the culture.
Demonstrates a firm grasp of stylistic nuances, irony, and humor.
Shows both global and detailed understanding of texts.
Understands almost all cultural references.
Reading speed is similar to that of a native speaker.

Literature Review

Clifford (2013, personal communication) defines reading comprehension as "the active, automatic, far-transfer process of using one's internalized language and culture expectancy system to efficiently comprehend an authentic text for the purpose for which it was written." He states that the reader at Level 4 understands meaning "beyond the lines." In other words, the reader is able to make evaluative judgements or express opinions about a text; evaluate the significance of the author's message, credibility, intent, and purpose; extrapolate beyond the text; and place it in a socio-cultural and historical context. Evaluative comprehension involves making a judgement about the text genre and mode of discourse, rhetorical organization of the text, and the writer's use of jargon, figures of speech, and allusions. Evaluative comprehension skills entail taking into account unstated assumptions in order to understand, evaluate, accept or reject the writer's arguments. While understanding "between the lines" is a required skill for both STANAG 6001 levels 3 and 4, understanding "beyond the lines" is a skill that distinguishes Level 4 from lower proficiency levels (STANAG 6001). It is also important to mention that attaining Distinguished or higher levels of language proficiency implies not only possessing outstanding language skills, but also higher order thinking skills, such as deductive and inductive reasoning, analysing, and synthesizing. Level 4 readers understand highly sophisticated written target language on unfamiliar general, abstract or professional-specialist topics. They generally understand specialized language on general abstract and complex topics outside of their area of expertise (e.g., philosophical essays written for a well-educated general reader). These readers can discern relationships among sophisticated written materials in the context of broad experience, and can follow unpredictable turns of thought in editorial, conjectural, and literary materials in any subject matter intended for the general reader. They also recognize, understand and usually correctly interpret cultural allusions, nuance and emotional overtones and attitudes (disenchantment, satire, humour, etc.) as well as less common figures of speech, such as malapropisms and spoonerisms.

Child (1998) elaborated on text difficulty and added that an author's unique point of view, and the method of argumentation may be complex and innovative at higher levels of proficiency. According to Lowe (1998), Level 4 texts are "abstract & culturally dense, often have embedding syntax used with virtuosity," while Edwards (1996, 19) states that the author "may take a novel or creative approach to a problem" adding that "in these texts, the reader is likely to encounter highly individualized or culture-specific forms of discourse, abstract metaphors, and symbolism. The author assumes a great deal of reader input and leaves historical, cultural or other references and assumptions unexplained.

Full comprehension of such texts goes beyond the literal comprehension of explicitly stated information. It involves interpretation and critical evaluation of the text and the authorial intention. By evaluating the text, the readers "enter into a dialogue with the text and make the text their own" (Alschuler et al, 2002, 6).

As valid and reliable testing involves accurate elicitation and rating procedures (Alschuler et al, 2002), the working group felt that only constructed response (CR) task types would be appropriate to elicit evidence of reading comprehension. At this level, multiple-choice questions, as a testing technique might become a puzzle or a riddle-solving exercise as the options would tend to become exceedingly convoluted, and too close in meaning to each other. Justification for adopting CR was also found in Shrock & Coscarelli's (2007) analysis of the cognitive abilities associated with proficiency levels (Figure 1) and the corresponding appropriateness of task types.

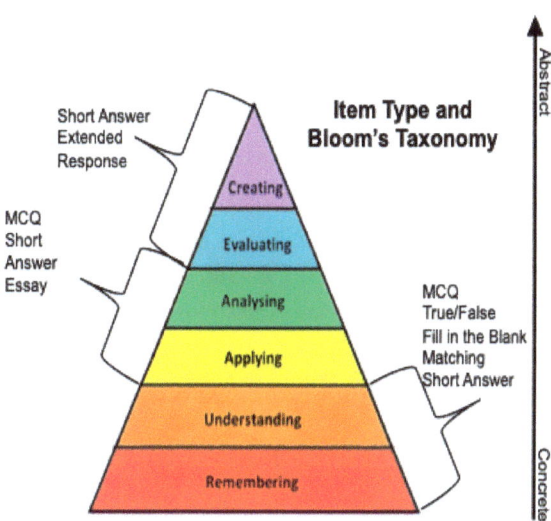

Fig. 1: Task types and cognitive abilities (Shrock & Coscarelli, 2007)

However, using CR task types at this level poses challenges in determining a suite of acceptable responses at a level where "reading entails a cognitive process which involves not only language and reading skills, but also general intellectual reasoning" (Aschuler et al, 2002). Additionally, in these reading tasks, "shared information and assumptions are at a minimum (and) personal input is paramount" (Child, 1998, 6). This places exponentially increased demands on raters (Child, 1998, 22).

Another layer of challenge lies in the possibility of test-takers' offering a variety of new interpretations of the text that may be plausible and thereby acceptable. In turn, raters themselves tend to have various interpretations of the test-takers' responses if the responses fall out of the fully acceptable or fully unacceptable ranges.

To address the complexities of rating CR at Level 4 and to determine a minimally acceptable performance or threshold level on the reading-comprehension prototype test, the WG adopted a novel standard setting approach the authors called the Retrodictive Modelling Approach (RMA), in which raters' conceptual understanding of Level 4 proficiency was triangulated with the patterns which emerged from their analytical ratings. These sessions were conducted in plenary and online using email and Qualtrics surveys. The authors, as group leaders, were responsible for collating and analyzing the patterns. In turn, the cut score yielded was further validated through multiple rounds of ratings where samples were recoded and anonymized, and qualitative evidence in the form of surveys collected from the raters.

Most standard setting methods rely on the expertise of the "judges" involved, in terms of familiarity with the test, understanding of the inferences and decisions made on the test scores, and conceptualization of how minimal criteria of performance might be exemplified (Angoff, 1971).

Kane (1998), claims that there is no real cut score to be found, but that rather the cut score needs to be created on the basis of many assumptions, the most important among these being the test purpose. Notwithstanding, determining the cut score may be fraught with issues stemming from the validity and reliability of the test itself (Dwoning et al, 1997), the examiners, (Schmitt et al, 1990), e.g. leniency/strictness, etc., the examinees, e.g. internal and external reliability issues deriving from concentration, health, psychological state, etc. Very similarly, the principles underpinning the RMA method lie on the assumption that the 'judges' are well-versed with the STANAG 6001 proficiency descriptors, understand the inferences made on the test scores, and are able to conceptualize what a threshold performance would look like in real world scenarios.

Statement of the Problem and Research Questions

As testimony to the challenges of establishing meaningful categories of those who meet the standards and those who do not, is the fact there is no "golden" standard setting method but rather a suite of over 400 methods that stakeholders may choose from for the purposes of their test project. Most methods focus on establishing pass/fail judgements (Cizek et al, 2007). Similarly, the RMA aims to determine two categories of test takers using empirical evidence as to whether individual responses to items meet the criteria at Level 4 with respect to judges' evaluations of successful, unsuccessful or partial responses in combination with qualitative judgments, based on a holistic evaluation of the test taker's performance being at Level 4 or not. The analysis of both approaches will yield a comparison of a patterned profile made up of the minimal number of successful (S), unsuccessful (U) and partial (P) responses which consistently correspond to the judges' holistic evaluation of a passing performance.

The RMA approach was applied to the STANAG 6001 Level 4 reading - to - write prototype test and its effectiveness was trialled on sample papers submitted by a selected cohort of test takers, thought to be Level 4 readers based on evaluative judgments made by teachers, currently held positions requiring such level, or prior national test scores. This paper intends to answer the following questions about the RMA approach, and its effectiveness to establish cut scores on a CR test in order to assess Distinguished levels of reading proficiency, in accordance with STANAG 6001 Level 4.

RQ1: *Does the threshold performance, identified through the RMA, accurately reflect the construct of STANAG 6001 Level 4 reading prototype test and validity of uses and interpretations that can be made on the basis of the test scores?*

RQ2: *How do judges' holistic evaluations correlate with their analytical scores, and how reliable are they in predicting the threshold performances*?

Method

Test Design and Development

The testing format selected was an integrated skills approach, i.e., reading tested via writing. Considering the challenges of choosing the appropriate test item type discussed earlier, a CR would enable the test taker to provide answers to complex questions, which characterize Level 4 reading texts, and which require the use of higher order thinking skills. Although the skill of writing was not tested *per se*, the WG felt that test takers would need to possess level 3 writing proficiency at a minimum, to be able to demonstrate comprehension of Level 4 texts.

The test format is thus a single-level test comprised of two authentic reading texts, each approximately 1400 words long. One text deals with a topic from the military doctrine field, and the other with a social/political issue. Both texts are intended for general educated readers, i.e., with no particular special area of expertise, or educational background. Each text is followed by six items, written in English and testing different Level 4 reading tasks, as per the STANAG 6001 descriptor, e.g., understand the author's choice of words in relation to the tone and persuasive stance/attitude, link ideas from various parts of the text, interpret the text in its wider cultural and societal context, follow unpredictable turns of thought, understand cultural references and allusions, etc. Paragraphs in each text are numbered, as tasks/questions may refer to a particular paragraph or to the text as a whole. One example of a Level 4 text and task is given below:

Excerpt from "Politics among Nations" *by Hans J. Morgenthau*

[Para 1] When one reflects upon the development of American thinking on foreign policy, one is struck by the persistence of mistaken attitudes that have survived- under whatever guises - both intellectual argument and political experience.

[Para 2] Once that wonder, in true Aristotelian fashion, has been transformed into the quest for rational understanding, the quest yields a conclusion both comforting and disturbing: we are here in the presence of intellectual defects shared by all of us in different ways and degrees. Together they provide the outline of a kind of pathology of international politics. When the human mind approaches reality with the purpose of taking action, of which the political encounter is one of the outstanding instances, it is often led astray by any of four common mental phenomena: residues of formerly adequate modes of thought and action now rendered obsolete by a new social reality; demonological interpretations of reality which substitute a fictitious reality - peopled by evil persons rather than seemingly intractable issues - for the actual one; refusal to come to terms with a threatening state of affairs by denying it through illusory verbalization; reliance upon the infinite malleability of a seemingly obstreperous reality.

[Para 3] Man responds to social situations with repetitive patterns. The same situation, recognized in its identity with previous situations, evokes the same response. The mind, as it were, holds in readiness a number of patterns appropriate for different situations; it then requires only the identification of a particular case to apply to it the preformed pattern appropriate to it. Thus, the human mind follows the principle of economy of effort, obviating an examination de novo of each individual situation and the pattern of thought and action appropriate to it. Yet when matters are subject to dynamic change, traditional patterns are no longer appropriate; they must be replaced by newness reflecting such change. Otherwise, a gap will open between traditional patterns and new realities, and thought and action will be misguided.

Sample Test Question (Whole Text): In the realm of international politics, what intellectual failings and attitudes do the Americans exhibit, and what are their origins?

Sample Response: When it comes to foreign policy and international politics the Americans tend to rely on obsolete views and allow their action to be guided by the principles that are no longer applicable to the newly arisen circumstances. Instead of adapting their views to the new realities and examining every new political situation with a fresh view, they misinterpret it by viewing it through the prism of either illusory perception or substituting that reality.

No specific instructions are given to the test takers as to the expected length of the response, except that it should be as complete, concise and coherent as possible. During the rating procedure, it was observed that some responses, albeit cryptic still showed clear evidence of comprehension, while some longer ones showed the opposite. Access to a pen and paper for note-taking was part of the administration procedure.

A complete guide to rating, including sample responses, was provided to all raters involved in the RMA piloting.

The Retrodictive Modelling Approach (RMA)

The WG members were experienced test developers and experts, who were all well-versed with the STANAG 6001 scale proficiency descriptors. Their professional background within the military context ensured full understanding of the inferences which would be made on test scores used for the purposes of this advanced proficiency level test. Two members of the working group had also participated in the development of this test, whereas the others had moderated or revised the multiple versions of the test before official piloting.

A tester booklet, containing the texts, administrative notes and instructions for the test takers, the rating process, as well as the sample responses (answer key), was provided to all raters within the WG. Each sample response, as per the above given example, specified the Level 4 reading task it was testing and the paragraph it referred to. The first rounds of ratings of the piloted tests included awarding an initial holistic score based on the STANAG 6001 Level 4 descriptor, and a detailed analytical score, reported as "Successful", "Unsuccessful" and "Partially successful." The latter option was included for those responses which did not fully match the ones in the answer key, but that, nonetheless, demonstrated that the test taker comprehended the question, and therefore the text to some extent. Proficiency levels in criterion-referenced tests based on STANAG 6001 are ranges of language performances. Test takers need to demonstrate mastery of language tasks within the content domains, and the accuracy demands of the level. Compensatory language behaviour, such as, for example, a test taker's aggregated and cumulative correct responses on a multi-level test cannot correspond to a proficiency level. Only a minimum number of correct responses at each level can determine mastery, or sustainment of performance.

To the extent that test developers strive to minimize the impact of extraneous, unpredictable and construct-irrelevant variables such as random reliability issues on test scores, these are nevertheless present (Davis, 2003).

Given that this reading test prototype is a mono-level test, and the broad spectrum of content domains and language functions it purports to measure in accordance with STANAG 6001 descriptors for reading comprehension, it is virtually impossible for test takers to get 100% correct answers on any given proficiency test (perhaps possible on an achievement test based solely on predictable curriculum content), raters decided to allow credit for partial answers to be factored in.

The scoring criteria, as outlined below, were developed as an analytical approach to rating. For the rating of the speaking and the writing skills, analytical ratings have been developed within the BILC community; however, none existed for the receptive skills. The intent with the criteria below was to design a simple analytical framework, pilot it and attempt to correlate the scores with the Level 4 descriptor by assigning a final holistic rating.

> **SUCCESSFUL** The examinee addressed the task and sub-tasks (if applicable) and he/her response either reflected fully the ideas expressed in the Sample response or provided another acceptable interpretation of the text. The response was sufficiently elaborate, precise and coherent.
>
> **PARTIAL** The examinee's answer did not fully address the task or it captured part of the basic idea(s) or details conveyed in the Sample Response. Even though the response was written with precise and coherent language, its content only partially corresponded to that given in the Sample Response.
>
> **UNSUCCESSFUL** The examinee's answer deviated from the information contained in the Sample Response showing a lack of comprehension of the text. It was written in a simple and concrete manner that did not convey the basic ideas contained in the Sample response.

Determining a minimally acceptable performance, or cut score was exceptionally challenging in this type of test, which integrated the two linguistic skills – reading and writing. Establishing two meaningful categories of those candidates who had met the criteria of sustained ability to understand a Level 4 reading passage via the modality of writing – even though their writing ability was not assessed per se'

– and those who did not was a fundamental aspect of the WG's tasks. The authors believe the RMA can be adopted to help establish these categories. The approach relies heavily on the expertise of the raters, who must be familiar with the STANAG scale, be familiar with the test itself, and with the inferences and decisions made on the test takers in conjunction with their inferred proficiency in the real world.

Given the high proficiency level being assessed, and the unique characteristics of Level 4 individualistic texts (Lowe,1998, 358), it is virtually impossible to anticipate all the possible responses candidates might be able to produce, which could nevertheless be evaluated as either partially or fully correct.

Flipping the rating process from the predictive to the retrodictive method offered raters a new assessment perspective and procedure. In order to establish the cut score, the working group believed that the five raters were the most suitable "judges" for the standard setting sessions (Angoff, 1971). Starting from a conceptualization of what the raters deemed a Level 4 reader could do, albeit minimally and correlating this evaluation with a more analytical assessment of the individual items was thought to yield a minimum profile of a threshold performance, which included the least number of successful, partial and unsuccessful responses, and which reflected the construct of Level 4 reading comprehension. The raters created this approach, the Retrodictive Modelling Approach (RMA), which aims to exemplify the criterial level of performance reflecting the Level 4 construct; it is a mixed, evidence-based rating process through which performances are assessed in three rating steps. The three rating steps needed to establish rating patterns, which would yield a minimum cut score, are outlined below:

- Step 1 - **Initial Holistic Rating (IHR)**: Raters read all responses globally, compare their overall impression of performance against the STANAG 6001 Level 4 descriptor, and mark their rating as "At Level" or "Below Level" for each individual item/task. The assumption is that all raters involved in this process have a clear theoretical concept of a Level 4 reader – at least holistically;

- Step 2 - **Analytic Rating-(AR)**: Raters analyse the responses individually by comparing them against the sample responses (answer key), and marking them as **Successful (S), Partial (P),** or **Unsuccessful (U)**;

- Step 3 - **Final Holistic Rating (FHR)**: Raters decide whether the test is a **PASS** at Level 4 by awarding it a final holistic rating that reflects the ranges of reading proficiency in accordance with STANAG 6001 Level 4 descriptor.

All tests were coded and the samples rated by five judges. When the initial holistic rating matched the final holistic rating, for example, a rating of "pass" (i.e.

candidate is deemed a Level 4 proficient reader), the authors analysed the analytical ratings to determine patterns of ratings, which emerged in terms of a specific number of successful, unsuccessful, and partial evaluations. The minimum number of "successful" scores for this profile, which consistently represented a match between the IHR and FHR would tentatively reflect the cut score.

The objective of the RMA-based rating method is to assist raters in the qualitative conceptualization of Level 4 reading proficiency in accordance with STANAG 6001. Employing this approach and forming a conceptual model of Level 4 (Distinguished) proficiency also enabled the WG to develop *a posteriori* rating criteria and establish the MAC.

The RMA procedure included:

1. norming sessions to agree on text and item levels (calibration);
2. norming sessions to agree on acceptable responses;
3. matching responses to the descriptor;
4. identifying patterns of performances at different ranges within the same level (threshold, mid, high);
5. analysing raters' scores on the performance grids;
6. trialling the scoring on actual responses.

The model retrospectively analyses patterns in the analytical scores, which correspond to raters' holistic evaluation of Level 4 (Distinguished) proficiency. The minimum common denominators, which are a combination of the Successful (S), Partial (P), and Unsuccessful (U) ratings or scores ultimately yield a minimally acceptable profile, which still corresponds to the WG's conceptualization of a threshold Level 4 reader.

Participants

The test was piloted in three phases, on a total of 38 candidates, a mix of military (N=32) and civilians (N=6), native (N=3) and non-native readers (N=35). The main piloting which involved 18 test takers took place at the International Military Staff (IMS), NATO Headquarters in Brussels, Belgium. All trialled test papers were rated remotely in three rounds: (a) an initial round during which a preliminary calibration and validation of the answer key were established; (b) a second, where the raters rated independently, and then submitted their results to the authors, and (c) a third, final round, where the established cut score was applied in order to validate its effectiveness in reflecting the construct. All samples were anonymized and labelled "sample A," "sample B," etc for each round of ratings, and they were also typed to facilitate reading.

A survey was created so that raters could record their evaluations. A box for comments was made available at the end of each sample for raters to add comments and observations about the samples, the ratings or the procedure, including the initial holistic score and its confirmation after having rated analytically.

Trialling the test included recruiting volunteers who were on active duty in international positions, which had been labelled by NATO stakeholders as requiring Level 4 proficiency. Local proctors ensured that the test was trialled in secure environments and specific instructions were given to both the test takers and the proctors. A test control officer from Belgium administered the test at NATO HQ to 15 test takers, and the Chief of Testing at SHAPE administered the test to 5 test takers. Subsequent trialling was conducted on 18 test takers, out of whom three were located at Supreme Allied Command Transformation (SACT), Norfolk, four at the Defence Military College in Sweden, three at the Defence Military College in Denmark, three at the Canadian Defence Academy, one at the Netherlands Defence Academy, three at Bundessprachenamt, Germany, and one at a private university on the East Coast, USA.

The rating process of the initial trials included applying the RMA process. In the meantime, test items/tasks were modified based on the analysis of the initial 18 test administrations. Raters were asked to provide an Initial Holistic Rating (IHR), and then proceed to rating the individual items (N=12) of the two texts. Subsequently, a Final Holistic Rating (FHR) would either confirm the initial holistic rating, or reject it given the analytic evidence of the individual items evaluated.

Results were compiled and a tentative cut score of 7 Successful 5 Partial and 2 Unsuccessful responses emerged that consistently reflected raters' understanding of STANAG Level 4 reading proficiency at its threshold/minimum level. Once the tentative cut score had been identified, an additional round of ratings was conducted by applying the newly established cut score (7S, 5P and 2U). Raters followed the above-described three-step rating process: 1) provide an IHR; 2) rate analytically; 3) provide a FHR. A box for comments was provided in which raters could elaborate on whether their holistic rating had changed based on the cut score.

Statistical tests and analysis

A FACETS analysis was run by considering the three facets of examinees, raters and test items. In order to do this, all Successful, Unsuccessful and Partial responses were converted to 2, 0 and 1, respectively. Similarly, the twelve examinee samples were coded A, B, C, D, G, J, K, L, N, R, S, T while the names of the raters were referred to as, rater 1, rater 2, rater 3, rater 4 and rater 5. Although the actual test comprised of two texts with six items each, the authors considered twelve items in the analysis as the initial holistic rating and the final holistic rating were each considered as additional items, for a total of 14 items. They were coded a T1 (referring to first of the two texts) and 1 (referring to the first item of that text so that T1_1 would refer to the first item of text 1 and T2_2 would refer to the second item of the second text and so on).

The examinees were considered as the "floating" facet whereby the greater the score, the greater the ability of the examinee. Instead, the rater facet analysis was run to determine the inter and intra rater reliability. An initial observation of the *fit* statistics shows the variability in rater harshness or leniency with a strong indication of rater self-consistency. This would lead to the importance of always having two raters in the rating process, which is consistent with best practices in test development projects.

Total Score	Total Count	Obsvd Average	Fair(M) Average	- Model Measure S.E.	Infit MnSq ZStd	Outfit MnSq ZStd	|Estim.| Discrm	Correlation PtMea PtExp	Exact Agree. Obs % Exp %	N Raters
147	144	1.02	1.07	-.53 .12	1.22 1.9	1.37 1.9	.63	.50 .63	59.0 53.7	5 rater 5
134	144	.93	.93	-.35 .12	.88 -1.1	.80 -1.1	1.11	.68 .63	68.6 55.3	2 rater 2
112	144	.78	.69	-.03 .12	.92 -.6	.81 -1.0	1.19	.68 .64	70.1 57.0	3 rater 5
105	144	.73	.62	.08 .12	.82 -1.5	.67 -1.8	1.28	.72 .63	76.2 57.2	4 rater 4
61	144	.42	.25	.84 .14	1.26 1.7	1.17 .6	.74	.47 .58	62.8 55.5	1 rater 1
111.8	144	.78	.71	.00 .13	1.02 .1	.96 -.3		.61		Mean (Count: 5)
29.5	.0	.21	.28	.47 .01	.18 1.5	.26 1.4		.10		S.D. (Population)
33.0	.0	.23	.32	.53 .01	.21 1.7	.29 1.5		.12		S.D. (Sample)

Model, Populn: RMSE .13 Adj (True) S.D. .46 Separation 3.65 Strata 5.20 Reliability (not inter-rater) .93

Model, Sample: RMSE .13 Adj (True) S.D. .52 Separation 4.11 Strata 5.81 Reliability (not inter-rater) .94

Model, Fixed (all same) chi-square: 63.3 d.f.: 4 significance (probability): .00

Model, Random (normal) chi-square: 3.8 d.f.: 3 significance (probability): .29

Inter-Rater agreement opportunities: 1440 Exact agreements: 970 = 67.4% Expected: 802.5 = 55.7%

The *fit* statistics of the test items are also within parameters although the items are reliably different from each other. There is evidence that the items might range in terms of "difficulty" or "ease". This finding is consistent with the conceptual framework of the STANAG 6001 scale whereby each level is a threshold level within a range of proficiency which is wider as the scale progresses, e.g. level 1 range is much narrower compared to the Level 4 range in terms of content, task, accuracy expectations and text type. The easiest item is the third item of text 2, with a logit of -1.52 whereas the harshest is item 2 of text 2 with a logit of 1.05. Furthermore, the final holistic rating was more stringent than the initial holistic rating, indicating that the analytical scores led to a negative final holistic score.

Total Score	Total Count	Obsvd Average	Fair(M) Average	Model Measure	Model S.E.	Infit MnSq	Infit ZStd	Outfit MnSq	Outfit ZStd	Estim. Discrm	Correlation PtMea	PtExp	Nu	Text_Item
88	60	1.47	1.63	-1.40	.19	1.18	1.0	1.25	.7	.86	.41	.51	9	T2_3
73	60	1.22	1.34	-.89	.18	1.12	.8	1.00	.1	1.28	.57	.57	5	T1_5
56	60	.93	.93	-.36	.18	.83	-1.0	.79	-.8	1.06	.67	.61	7	T2_1
56	60	.93	.93	-.36	.18	.81	-1.2	.65	-1.5	1.53	.74	.61	11	T2_5
48	60	.80	.74	-.10	.18	.71	-1.8	.79	-.7	.68	.64	.61	12	T2_6
45	60	.75	.66	.01	.19	1.45	2.2	1.60	2.0	.43	.36	.61	6	T1_6
44	60	.73	.64	.04	.19	.73	-1.5	.69	-1.2	1.17	.71	.61	1	T1_1
42	60	.70	.59	.11	.19	1.18	1.0	1.37	1.2	.80	.51	.61	3	T1_3
33	60	.55	.40	.45	.20	1.13	.6	1.23	.7	.84	.50	.59	4	T1_4
29	60	.48	.33	.62	.21	1.14	.7	.90	-.1	1.00	.55	.58	2	T1_2
26	60	.43	.27	.76	.22	1.10	.5	.89	-.1	.93	.52	.56	10	T2_4
19	60	.32	.18	1.12	.24	.75	-1.0	.39	-1.4	1.41	.69	.51	8	T2_2
46.6	60.0	.78	.72	.00	.19	1.01	.0	.96	-.1		.57			Mean (Count: 12)
18.9	.0	.32	.42	.67	.02	.22	1.3	.33	1.1		.11			S.D. (Population)
19.8	.0	.33	.43	.70	.02	.23	1.3	.34	1.1		.12			S.D. (Sample)

Model, Populn: RMSE .20 Adj (True) S.D. .65 Separation 3.30 Strata 4.74 Reliability .92
Model, Sample: RMSE .20 Adj (True) S.D. .68 Separation 3.46 Strata 4.95 Reliability .92
Model, Fixed (all same) chi-square: 133.6 d.f.: 11 significance (probability): .00
Model, Random (normal) chi-square: 10.2 d.f.: 10 significance (probability): .43

The *fit* statistics of the examinees shows that most are within a normal range of .5 – 1.5. Examinee A is an outlier as their *fit* statistics are 1.83: at a closer look, raters do not seem to follow the pattern in using the 0 rating (i.e. unsuccessful). Overall, the reliability is .96 which is a strong indicator that the examinees are at different levels of ability. Since this is a mono-level test, it might point to the difficulty of the actual items.

Total	Total	Obsvd	Fair(M)|	+	Model	Infit		Outfit		|Estim.|	Correlation		
Score	Count	Average	Average	Measure	S.E.	MnSq	ZStd	MnSq	ZStd	|Discrm|	PtMea PtExp	Nu Examinees
16	60	.27	.17	-1.58	.24	1.02	.1	.68	-.5	1.30	.54 .41	7 K
21	60	.35	.24	-1.32	.22	.84	-.6	.84	-.2	.72	.37 .45	10 R
25	60	.42	.30	-1.14	.21	.56	-2.4	.52	-1.4	.96	.62 .47	12 T
26	60	.43	.31	-1.09	.20	.86	-.6	.70	-.8	1.29	.60 .47	11 S
30	60	.50	.38	-.94	.19	1.29	1.4	1.33	1.0	1.22	.46 .49	4 D
35	60	.58	.47	-.76	.19	.86	-.7	.86	-.4	.91	.53 .51	8 L
38	60	.63	.53	-.66	.18	.90	-.6	.95	.0	.72	.47 .52	2 B
44	60	.73	.65	-.47	.18	1.31	1.9	1.31	1.2	1.26	.47 .53	9 N
66	60	1.10	1.14	.18	.17	.95	-.2	.82	-.8	1.74	.67 .54	5 G
73	60	1.22	1.29	.38	.17	.82	-1.2	.86	-.5	.44	.48 .53	6 J
92	60	1.53	1.65	1.02	.20	1.89	3.8	1.89	2.2	.79	.15 .47	1 A
93	60	1.55	1.67	1.06	.20	.77	-1.2	.80	-.5	.63	.42 .47	3 C
46.6	60.0	.78	.73	-.44	.20	1.01	-.1	.96	-.1		.48	Mean (Count: 12)
26.2	.0	.44	.53	.86	.02	.33	1.6	.36	1.0		.13	S.D. (Population)
27.4	.0	.46	.55	.89	.02	.35	1.7	.37	1.1		.14	S.D. (Sample)

Model, Populn: RMSE .20 Adj (True) S.D. .83 Separation 4.24 Strata 5.99 Reliability .95
Model, Sample: RMSE .20 Adj (True) S.D. .87 Separation 4.44 Strata 6.25 Reliability .95
Model, Fixed (all same) chi-square: 216.0 d.f.: 11 significance (probability): .00
Model, Random (normal) chi-square: 10.5 d.f.: 10 significance (probability): .40
Table 1 Examinees Measurement Report(arranged by MN).

The probability curves found show that successful and unsuccessful (2 and 0) facets cross, whereas partials (i.e. 1) are not functioning as a category because the rating is not used quite as often by the raters (13% of times).

The above-illustrated results help to answer the research questions about the effectiveness of the RMA. As this was a pilot study, and there is not a copious body of literature identifying best practices and standard setting methods to establish threshold performances in high stakes, high-level proficiency testing in STANAG 6001-based testing, the main objective and rationale of this conceptual paper was to provide a standard setting method, which would exemplify minimal performance that reflected reading comprehension proficiency in accordance with the STANAG 6001 descriptor. Hence, it was important for the working group members, as representatives of the most well-versed experts in STANAG 6001 Level 4 proficiency, to agree and advance a common understanding and conceptualization of the cut score, and its reflection of the construct.

Discussion of Results

RQ1: *Does the threshold performance, identified through the RMA, accurately reflect the construct of STANAG 6001 Level 4 reading prototype test and validity of uses and interpretations that can be made on the basis of the test scores?*

Both the quantitative analysis using FACETS and the standard setting sessions among the raters show that partial ratings do not contribute significantly to evaluating the responses and determining whether a test taker has fully met the requirements of a Level 4 reader. This could be due to a psychological factor whereby the rater would rather opt for an unsuccessful rating if the examinee's response does not fully meet expectations. STANAG 6001 is a non-compensatory proficiency scale and sustained ability across the three dimensions of content, task and accuracy per level must be demonstrated by a test-taker in order to be awarded that particular level. All raters were well-versed with the STANAG 6001 descriptors, with the test and with the purpose the scores would have in this highly specialized context. However, the non-compensatory nature of the scale may have influenced the raters into awarding more successful and unsuccessful ratings compared to partial ratings. Given the high -stakes nature of this type of context, raters may have preferred to err towards under compensating rather than giving the benefit of the doubt to a response.

RQ2: *How do judges' holistic evaluations correlate with their analytical scores and how reliable are they in predicting the threshold performances?*

As the pre and post ratings show, there is a high inter and intra-rater reliability between initial holistic ratings and final holistic ratings when the cut score identified through the RMA was applied. This denotes consistency within and among the raters, and confirms raters' conceptualization of what it means to be a STANAG 6001 Level 4 reader, based on their experience with the scale, with the test and, mostly, with the inferences and decisions which can potentially be made based on the test scores. Given the high stakes, it is a proven best practice in test development and administration to always have two raters who agree on a rating.

Conclusion

Any approach to setting standards must entail extensive trialling and thorough consequential validity studies to confirm that the minimum cut score established validly reflects the test purpose and use. The RMA approach was applied to scoring test responses of only thirty-three examinees. A major limitation of this study is the sample size which does not allow to make any generalizable inferences of the effectiveness of the method. Further trialling, along with studies of consequential and scoring validity should be conducted to add significant information about the approach's effectiveness. A statistically significant number of participants, who would be able to pilot the test and the scoring method would be required in order to be able to generalize the appropriateness and applicability of the RMA to official, national testing of Level 4 reading proficiency in accordance with STANAG 6001. Furthermore, additional, external information about the participants' reading proficiency would help to correlate findings with the RMA and determine concurrent validity of the present test design (reading to write).

Finally, further research is needed to comprehend the construct of reading at such high (Distinguished) levels of proficiency, and determine which testing technique best captures such comprehension. Scoring methods reflect the construct and only investigating the true nature of such a construct at this level would be conducive to a valid and reliable cut score setting.

This conceptual paper aims to illustrate a novel approach to setting cut scores which combines the holistic evaluation of expert raters and the analytical ratings of individual constructed responses, called the Retrodictive Modelling Approach on a high-stakes proficiency test. A pattern of minimal combinations of S, U and P ratings, analysed in conjunction with the consistent ratings of initial and final holistic ratings would then yield a cut score. This project shows how important it is to have expert raters on subjectively-scored responses, and that there should always be two raters, if not more, in case of discrepancy in judgment. Rating should initially be done individually and then compared to a second rater's evaluation. Another important finding is the fact that analytical scoring contributes to guide the rater as to whether the final rating should be changed from the initial rating. A holistic rating alone does not seem to consistently predict the performance of the sample.

This project is far from over. Consequential validity studies which investigate the consistent and meaningful uses of the cut score found through the RMA needs further research within and across NATO member and partner neations which have adopted the STANAG 6001 proficiency scale and need to test Level 4 proficiency.

Acknowledgements

This project would not have been possible without the tireless support of Ms. Peggy Garza (U.S. Marshall Center, Germany) and Mr. Keith Wert (U.S. Marshall Center, Germany), BILC secretary and Chair at the time of this project. Additionally, special recognition must be given to the Working Group members who contributed to the project as either test developers or raters, and who devoted countless hours to this work: Ms Petya Georgieva (National Defense College, BLG), Ms Nancy Powers & Dr. May Tan (Military Personnel Generation Group, St., CAN), Mr. Käre Kildevang and Dr. Allen Christiansen (Royal Danish Defense College, DNK), Dr. Donald Sturges (Bundessprachennamt, GER), Mr. Gerard Seinhorst (National Defense Language Center, NL), Ms Annette Nolan & Mr. Keith Farr (Swedish Defense College, SWE), Mr. David Oglesby (U.S. Marshall Center, Germany), and Dr. Martha Herzog (DLIFLC, USA).

Finally, the authors wish to thank Dr. Troy Cox (BYU, USA) for his expertise and help along with Dr. Ray Clifford (BYU, USA) for his contribution to understanding Level 4 proficiency according to STANAG 6001.

References

Alschuler, C. & Moussa, N. (2002). *Testing reading at ILR Levels 4, 4+ and 5: A Tester Training Model*. Presentation to the Interagency Language Roundtable Committee, Foreign Service Institute, Washington, D.C.

Angoff, W. H. (1971). Scales, norms, and equivalent scores. In Thorndike, R.L. (Ed.), *Educational. Measurement* (pp. 508-600). American Council on Education.

Language Needs Analysis. (2015). Unpublished NATO BILC internal document.

Chang, L., Dziuban, C., Hynes, M., & Olson, A. (1996). Does a standard reflect minimal competency of examinees or judge competency?" *Applied Measurement in Education 9 (2)*: 161.

Child, J.R. (1998) Language skill levels, textual modes and the rating process. *Foreign Language Annals 3*: 381–397.

Cizek, G., & Bunch, M. (2007). *Standard-setting: A guide to establishing and evaluating performance standards on tests*. SAGE Publications.

Davis, A. (2003). Three heresies of language testing research. *Language Testing 20(4)*: 355–368. https:// 10.1191/0265532203lt263oa.

Downing, S. M., & Haladyna, T. M. (1997). Test item development: Validity evidence from quality assurance processes. *Applied Measurement in Education 10*: 61-82. https://doi:10.1207/s15324818ame1001_4.

Edwards, A. L. (1996). Reading proficiency assessment and the ILR/American Council on the teaching of foreign languages text typology: A reevaluation. *Modern Language Journal 80*: 350–361.

Kane, M. T. (1998). Criterion bias in examinee-centered standard setting: Some thought experiments. *Educational Measurement, Issues and Practice 17*: 23–30.

Lowe, P. (1998). Keeping the optic constant: A framework of principles for writing and specifying the AEI definitions of language abilities. *Foreign Language Annals, 31(3)*: 358–380.

Shrock, S. & Coscarelli, W. (2007). *Criterion-referenced test development. Technical and legal guidelines for corporate training (3rd edition)*. Internet: Pfeiffer & Company.

Shulruf, B., Poole, P., & Wilkinson, T. (2015), The Objective Borderline Method: A probabilistic method for standard setting, *Assessment & Evaluation in Higher Education 40(3)*: 420–438. https://dx.doi.org/10.1080/02602938.2014.918088.

Shin, S., & Lidster, R.(2017), Evaluating different standard-setting methods in an ESL placement testing context. *Language Testing 34(3)*: 357–381. https://DOI:10.1177/026553226646605.

Standardizing Agreement 6001 Proficiency Scale (STANAG). (2015). Unpublished BILC document. www.bilc.org.

Re-Conceptualizing Language Programs to Achieve Level 4

Christine Campbell, Campbell Language Consultats (USA)

Interagency Language Roundtable (ILR) Language Skill Level Descriptions, which delineate levels of proficiency using a scale from 0 through 5, can portray the individual at Level 4[43]. In the U.S., this level is sometimes referred to as "The Diplomat" by American Council on the Teaching of Foreign Languages (ACTFL, ILR Workshop, 2018): that is, one with access to a vast linguistic repertoire. Within the context of professional needs, such a person can understand all forms and styles of speech, read fluently and accurately all styles and forms of the language, and speak fluently and accurately on all levels. Scholars and practitioners who have written about learners either approaching or at this level highlight certain shared characteristics while recognizing their uniqueness (Davidson & Garas, 2018; Davidson & Shaw, 2019; Ehrman, 2002; Farraj, 2006; Ingold, 2002; Leaver, 2003; Leaver & Atwell, 2002; Leaver & Campbell, 2015, 2020; Leaver & Shekhtman, 2002; Robin, 2008; Soudakoff, 2004).

Recently, Franke (2020) conducted a qualitative case study that explored how persistence, study abroad, motivation, and learner autonomy play into the pursuit of Distinguished speaking proficiency in particular. The data analysis of interviews with the non-native speakers revealed that attaining Level 4 "was a highly personal pursuit, characterized by different motivations based on the choice of a foreign language, engagement in the target culture, grit, and time. Overall, the participants

---

[43] Level 4 in the ILR scale is equivalent to the Distinguished Level on the ACTFL Proficiency Guidelines scale. For more information, see www.govtilr.org and www.actfl. org/publications/guidelines-and-manuals/actfl. In the article, level references will be to both the ILR and the ACTFL scales at the start, then only to the former (cf. ILR/ACTFL).

were highly self-efficacious learners, many married to foreign-speaking spouses, and spent [sic] extended periods in the foreign culture and community" (p. iv).

Corin (2020) proposes that if learners are to have a realistic chance of reaching Level 4, the second language (L2) learning process must be designed in such a way that they can: 1) approach Level 3 early enough in the course of learning (typically, in their organized courses of study) to "enable an ascent" to the mountain summit--near-native proficiency; and 2) arrive at Level 3 already possessing specific "equipment," here understood as "expanded learning capacity," needed for the final scale to the top (pp. 1 and 25, respectively). The "capacity" is comprised of skills such as "strategic ambidexterity," including both preferred [learning] strategies [e.g., metacognitive, cognitive, social, affective, and communicative as per Shekhtman, 2003b] and those typical of learners with opposite 'native' learning styles, expanded sociocultural awareness, competencies and permeability" (p. 25).

This chapter will focus on a separate aspect of the Level 4 dialogue—concrete, proven measures that Level 4 language programs can take when re-conceptualizing. Specifically, it will describe actions implemented by the Directorate of Continuing Education (CE), Defense Language Institute Foreign Language Center (DLIFLC), from 2006 through 2016 to facilitate learners attaining high levels of proficiency in standardized exit tests—the *Defense Language Proficiency Test (DLPT)*, for Listening Comprehension (LC) and Reading Comprehension (RC) and the *Oral Proficiency Interview (OPI)*, for Speaking (SP). At the time, CE was responsible for teaching three types of courses, among others—Intermediate, Advanced, and Defense Threat Reduction Agency (DTRA) Interpreting[44].

The far-reaching goals to be Distinguished from graduation requirements of the Advanced and DTRA courses were Level 3+ and above in LC and RC and Level 3 and above in SP. Graduation requirements for the two courses were, and are still today, considerably less demanding: Advanced Course—Level 3 in LC and RC and Level 2 in Speaking (SP); DTRA—Level 2+ in LC and RC and Level 2 in SP. The entry requirement for the Advanced Course is Level 2+ in LC and RC; DTRA, Level 2 in LC and RC. There is no entry requirement in SP. The length of the Advanced Course is 19 weeks; DTRA, 47 weeks. Given the surprisingly low entry and graduation requirements, the consistently high scores historically achieved in the CE Program, the DTRA Course in particular, are especially noteworthy.

First, this article will review the institutional context of the CE language program. Then, it will study measures put in place to bring about fundamental change in curricular design, teacher education, and learner education (here understood as instruction in learner styles and strategies, orientations about pedagogical approaches and classroom protocol, etc.) as part of CE's quest to reach ever higher levels of proficiency. Finally, it will examine the DTRA Interpreting Course Program, where learners regularly attain Level 3+ and above in at least one of the three

---

44 The article narrative is set in the past given it relates to activities in CE from 2006-2016.

skills. At this point in 2020, for example, 63% of DTRA learners have graduated at Levels 3+ and 4 in at least one of the three skills[45].

The Institutional Context of the CE Language Program

DLIFLC is the premier language learning facility of the United States government, where close to 4,500 learners, the majority potential military linguists, study one of 17 languages. Its faculty of 1800 is comprised of teachers, curriculum developers, teacher educators, test developers, technology specialists, and more. Due to geopolitical security concerns facing the United States, DLIFLC was urged by the government in 2012 to re-look its *modus operandi* as part of an Institute-wide initiative designed to increase by 30% to 80%, depending on the language program, the number of graduating learners from the Basic Course (BC) at Level 2+ in LC and RC and Level 2 in SP.

The in-depth needs analysis conducted at the outset of the initiative ultimately led to a call for a different educational approach. To reach higher levels of proficiency, the approach would have to go beyond Communicative Language Teaching (CLT). Leaver, who became Provost of DLIFLC in 2013, had been applying principles of Transformative Learning (TL) which identifies "perspective transformation" as the central learning process, into her teaching since the 1990s (Mezirow, 2000, p. xi). Seeing the potential of TL for language learning, where learners are exposed to different perspectives on the realities of life as part of their language and culture studies, she disseminated its principles at the Institute, where they inform practices until today.

TL, according to its discoverer, Mezirow (2000), is "the process by which we transform our taken-for-granted frames of reference (meaning perspectives, habits of mind, mind-sets) to make them more inclusive, discriminating, open, emotionally capable of change, and reflective so that they may generate beliefs and opinions that will prove more true or justified to guide action…Frames of reference are the results of ways of interpreting experience" (pp. 7-8 and 16, respectively). He elaborates: "[W]e transform frames of reference—our own and those of others—by becoming critically reflective of their assumptions and aware of their context—the source, nature, and consequences of taken-for-granted beliefs" (p. 19). Individuals undergoing transformation pass through phases in which they "clarify meaning" as they experience the world (p. 22). The first phase—often a "disorienting dilemma," provokes self-examination and critical assessment of assumptions that lead to the exploration and adoption of new roles, relationships, and actions, which culminate in a "new perspective" (p. 22).

Widely discussed and applied in the field of adult education for over years, TL had received limited attention in world language education (e.g., Arce, 2000; Foster,

---

[45] More specific information is inaccessible for security reasons.

1997; Goulah, 2006; Leaver & Granoien, 2000; McClinton, 2005; Osterling & Webb, 2009) until more recently. In 2006, Leaver introduced select principles at CE; in 2013, she incorporated them as part of the Institute initiative to raise proficiency levels. Its formal adaptation to language learning as "Transformative Language Learning and Teaching" (TLLT) is the result of a collaborative effort by professionals such as Leaver, Davidson, and Campbell (2020) and Nyikos and Oxford (Leaver, Campbell, Nyikos, & Oxford, R., 2019).

The primary goals of TLLT are personal transformation that results in bilingual and bicultural competence and learner autonomy. Common features of TLLT as currently being used in diverse learning contexts include the following:

- "Materials and daily communications are authentic and unadapted, beginning at the earliest levels of instruction.

- The classroom is immersive. Immersion in-country reflects the typical life of the native speaker of the same age to the extent practicable.

- Personal transformation involves cognitive, emotional, and cultural shifts occurring within the individual: that is, developing self-awareness, resolving disorienting dilemmas, identifying cognitive distortions, managing emotions, and integrating two (or more) cultures on their own terms.

- Highly individualized programs are informed by learning styles and strategies and the "invisible classroom" emanating from inherent personality variables.

- Open architecture curricular design (OACD), a term taken from a parallel concept in computer design that allows for interchangeable parts, supports increasingly textbook-free classrooms as learners develop greater proficiency and teachers modify syllabi corresponding to learners' changing needs.

- The grading system uses formative assessments and feedback, with occasional summative assessments (projects, presentations, contracted assignments, and portfolios), that integrate outcome and process, instead of separating them.

- Programs empower learners to take charge of their own learning.

- Program design and supervisors empower teachers to take charge of their own classrooms as advisors, mentors, coaches, planners, and strategists (Leaver et al., 2020).

TLLT principles operate within a context that is grounded in the national standards (The National Standards Collaborative Board, 2019) and is content-based and learner-centered.

Contrasting TL with TLLT, Leaver posits: "At least for now, these types of TLLT activities differ in important ways from contemporary aspects of transformative learning in adult education: whereas transformative adult education often focuses on creating change in society, TLLT seeks to understand and create a synthesis with the other society" (p. 19, Leaver, 2020).

Due to the history of high scores attained by CE learners upon graduation, senior management at DLIFLC analyzed the CE program closely for practices that would transfer to the Basic Course. Although the learners were different in that those in CE were professional military linguists in their early and mid-20s and those in the BC were budding military linguists aged 18-21, the over-arching approach toward curricular design, teacher education, and learner education was deemed applicable. A description of the three areas follows.

Curricular Design

Many educators today who keep abreast of the latest developments in curricular design practice the "backward-design" principle of modern curricula, which Wiggins and McTighe (2005) posit starts with the performance goals and works backwards to the performance assessments,[46] whether formative or summative. Sandrock (2010) distills the principles of backward design like so: "[I]dentify clear performance goals, then create assessment tasks through which students will demonstrate the performance goals, and finally plan what students need to know and be able to do in order to be successful in the assessments—that is, the vocabulary, grammatical items, and language functions" (p. 170).

The backward-design principle is one aspect of Open Architecture Curricular Design (OACD), a fundamental feature of TLLT that was first introduced to CE faculty by Leaver in 2006. OACD is a flexible framework that encourages teacher–learner negotiation through the use of a theme-based syllabus (versus a textbook), generally beginning at Levels 1+/Intermediate High and above though there is evidence of the successful introduction of OACD at much lower levels (Clifford, 1988; Duri, 1992), depending on factors such as teacher and learner readiness. A fundamental principle of TLLT, OACD has been a critical factor in CE's academic successes.

---

46 In the language learning context, Sandrock (2010) confirms that performance assessments "provide a realistic description of expected student progress in developing proficiency in the language" (p. 171).

Below, measures taken to reconceptualize curricular design in CE:

Adopt OACD

Leaver, who had implemented aspects of OACD without using the term as early as the 1980s at the Foreign Service Institute (Leaver, 1989), shared it with faculty at CE when she assumed the position of Associate Provost in 2006. In OACD, a textbook orients teachers through Level 1/Intermediate Low and Intermediate Mid to facilitate standardization in the development of structural and lexical control. Generally beginning at Level 1+/Intermediate High and above, but occasionally at lower levels, depending on teacher and learner readiness, there is no textbook but rather a theme-based syllabus guiding teachers. Common features exhibited by OACD teachers are:

- use of authentic materials from day one;
- deliberate, continual use of the target language;
- learner delivery of content [From the start of instruction, there is ongoing learner involvement in both the delivery and selection of content];
- project/scenario-based instruction;
- development and use of higher-order thinking skills;
- use of formative assessments;
- integration of both formal and colloquial language;
- integration of non-standard language;
- incorporation of collaborative learning, such as group presentations and projects based on learner research;
- use of a wider variety of listening and reading genres across the full spectrum of social media platforms, such as Instagram, Twitter, WhatsApp, possibly Facebook, LinkedIn, blogs, and so on (Campbell & Sarac, 2017);
- systematic defossilization;
- focus on stylistics, including use of register;
- focus on discourse analysis;
- incorporation of super-authentic (Cohen, 2015) language – language spoken by two or more people with ambient noise, grammatical mistakes, fillers, and so on; and

- top-down and bottom-up processing of high-level presentations on topical domains such as politics, economics, and history by guest speakers (Campbell, 2020).

Redesign the Assessments

As Dabaneh and Yuan (2020) observe, "[o]ver the past four decades, testing specialists have pondered the role of testing and to what extent it can be "educative," informing learners about their strengths and weaknesses and preparing them for the next level of learning (Wiggins, 1998, cover)" (p. 1). The advent of task-based instruction brought about the deliberate integration of assessment and instruction, which in turn led to [instruction] "embedded assessment," defined in 2003 by Spence-Brown as "the use of tasks which serve a pedagogical purpose for assessment" and has the advantage of providing robust feedback and allowing for the washback effect to motivate students to achieve specific short term goals"(p. 36). According to this researcher, the problem with this type of "formative" assessment is that the product of learning "does not represent what a student can do unassisted, after the learning cycle is completed, but what they can do with support during the learning process" (p.36).

Also in 2003, Poehner and Lantolf, expanding on previous work, published "Dynamic Assessment of L2 Development: Bringing the Past into the Future," where they examine "Dynamic Assessment" (DA) as a developmental approach to assessment and instruction derived from Vygotsky's theory of the Zone of Proximal Development (ZPD). They define DA "as a procedure whose outcome takes into account the results of intervention. In the intervention, the examiner teaches the examinee how to perform better on individual items or on the test as a whole. The final score may be a learning score representing the difference between pretest (before learning) and posttest (after learning) scores, or it may be the score on the posttest considered alone" (pp. 1-2). In 2017, Poehner, Davin, and Lantolf reiterate that "[d]ynamic assessment, or DA, departs from the traditional distinction between formative and summative assessment, as it understands teaching to be an inherent part of all assessment regardless of purpose or context" (p. 243).

Outside of the DA context, the distinction between formative and summative assessments is generally observed. Perhaps Bachman's (1990) definition, cited by Poehner and Lantolf in 2005, is the most succinct: "In the language testing literature, FA [Formative Assessment] is usually contrasted with Summative Assessment on the grounds that the former is intended to feed back into the teaching and learning process while the latter reports on the outcomes of learning" (pp. 60–61)" (p. 233).

When redesigning assessments to focus on teaching versus testing, for example, it is critical to understand fully the differences between formative and summative assessments or a language program can perpetuate the over-testing trend found in many learning institutions. In *The Keys to Assessing Language Performance: A Teacher's Manual for Measuring Student Progress*, Sandrock (2010) provides a practitioner-oriented definition of the two, with helpful examples of each: "Formative assessment ranges from quick learning checks to activities guiding students to more independent use of language....In summative assessment, students demonstrate to themselves and their teacher that they can apply the lessons learned, the skills acquired, and the knowledge gained in the unit of instruction. This is when students produce language on their own and show what they are able to do as a result of the instruction. Summative assessment is a new application of the individual elements of vocabulary and grammar assessed at the formative level. Through summative assessment, students showcase the level of proficiency acquired" (pp. 62-64).

Balancing the two types of assessments, teachers are responsible for ensuring feedback is continually provided to learners. For Sandrock, feedback in formative assessment is "specific and highly focused, as students are learning and practicing various building blocks in preparation for the final unit level performances (e.g., commenting on pronunciation, use of a specific structure, or ability to elaborate and provide more detail). In summative assessment, feedback is more broad and holistic, where the teacher steps back and looks at the overall performance (e.g., commenting on student ability to get meaning across, maintain a conversation, or organize a strong argument)" (pp. 62-63).

Sandrock provides helpful examples of formative vs. summative assessments. Below, one of each:

Level: Level 0+, Emerging Level 1/Novice
Topic: What Makes a Good Friend? How Am I a Good Friend to Others?

"Formative Tasks:
- Ask other students what they like to do.
- Ask other students what they do to help others.
- In small groups, list characteristics of a good friend.
- Hear statements and identify if a good friend would or would not do that.
- List what friends do in school, what friends do outside of school.
- Write down two things you will do to be a better friend to others.

Summative Tasks:
- Listen to a conversation and on a list of things that good friends do, check off what these friends say they do for each other.
- Identify with a partner what good friends do and don't do.

- Write a letter to a friend identifying three things you plan to do as a good friend and three things you will not do as a good friend" (pp. 61-62).

Sandrock also highlights the role of rubrics when distinguishing formative from summative assessments like so: "Formative assessments, being simpler, shorter, and more limited in scope, may not necessarily require a rubric. Summative assessments elicit a more complex performance from students and therefore warrant the time needed to develop a rubric that can provide extensive feedback" (p. 88).

Informed by the developments in the assessment field like those reviewed above, in the mid 2000s CE revamped the entire assessment program to focus on formative assessments, with occasional summative ones. The re-conceptualizing led to the situation Sandrock describes in the conclusion to *Keys*: "When student progress is measured through performance assessment and effective feedback, students know what they can do in the new language they are acquiring and what they need to do to improve their proficiency and increase their confidence in using the three modes of communication. This is the road map to guide language teaching and learning" (pp. 190-191).

Teacher Education

Teacher education[47] is often recognized as perhaps the most significant factor in improving learner performance. Well-designed, task-based, content-based, learner-centered instruction informed by the world-readiness standards sets up optimal conditions for learning which learners can use to further their goals as autonomous persons. Below, measures taken to reconceptualize the CE Teacher Education Program:

Foster a Community of Understanding and Practice

Just as it is critical for learners and teachers in today's learning space to work together to create a learning community where both groups share an understanding of expectations and strive to reach the same goals, so it is crucial to forge the same kind community of understanding and practice among key participants in an educational setting (Bailey & Freeman, 1990). The community of participants, which includes learners, faculty, and administrators, can benefit from adopting a team approach to dealing with the challenges of a language program, whether an increase in learners not completing graduation requirements, an outdated or rigid curriculum, understaffing, a percentage of the faculty who is pedagogically unpre-

---

[47] Teacher education is interpreted broadly here to encompass both current classroom teachers and those who have joined the administration such as Deans, Department Chairs, and Team Leaders. (At DLIFLC, a teaching team model where two to six teachers collaborate daily on the creation [in some cases, only adaptation] of the curriculum, is used.)

pared, and more. The team approach is especially effective during times of change as it diffuses the anxiety often felt by participants.

In the case of CE, when Leaver brought aspects of TLLT such as OACD to the Directorate in 2006, the faculty were compelled to learn a new way of creating curricula and teaching. Understandably, changes in faculty performance standards due to the changes in pedagogical orientation caused anxiety. The team approach facilitated the creation of a community of participants who rallied to meet the new requirements. The premise of the approach is that all participants share in program successes and failures. Successes were celebrated; failures were opportunities to learn. When, for example, learners did not meet the minimum graduation requirements in standardized exit tests, the administration first recognized the efforts of the conscientious faculty who had put forth every effort to succeed. Then, the administration and faculty held meetings to discuss and document what worked and what did not. Learners, accustomed to voicing their perspectives with the administration and faculty in periodic "Sensing Sessions," which are described in detail in the "Learner Education" section below, shared their comments in focus groups. The information gathered at the meetings and focus groups was included in a report that acted as a guide for future courses so course strengths could be enhanced and weaknesses eliminated.

The team approach was also used when crafting the in-service Teacher Education Program. Several times per month, two to three faculty made presentations about relevant language learning issues as part of the Professional Development Series held after the class day from 3:30-4:30 p.m. The Series was organized by faculty for faculty.

Set High Expectations

Goethe, the 18th century author, stated about expectations: "Treat people as if they were what they ought to be, and you help them to become what they are capable of being" (https://quoteinvestigator.com/2018/10/09/capable/). The CE community of participants has consistently confronted challenges, such as the setting of higher expectations, with optimism and fortitude, knowing they are supported by an organizational culture that promotes teamwork. For example, when new performance standards were issued in CE in 2007 due to the changes in pedagogical approach made by Leaver, the community adapted to the higher expectations, understanding that each community member would accept a greater degree of responsibility. They reacted similarly when the new graduation goals in the BC—80% 2+ in LC and RC by 2021—were announced by DLIFLC in 2013. Although CE does not teach the BC, the higher percentages of 2+/2+ meant that CE had to graduate learners in the Intermediate Course at higher levels, and, as a consequence, the Advanced Course took on even higher goals. Today, the CE community continues to display the same flexibility and dedication.

Redesign the Teacher Observation Program

Regarding teacher observations, the Institute requires Chairs to conduct several summative ones, where information gathered is used to inform the annual teacher performance evaluation. CE re-designed the teacher observation system with a focus on the formative value of observations, converting a typically anxiety-provoking event into an opportunity to re-visit one's strengths and learn how to improve areas of concern. Chairs announced the formative observations, emphasizing that information collected would be used solely as a reflection tool for teachers. Faculty members were also urged to conduct peer-to-peer teacher observations.

Promote Access to Institute-Wide Professional Development Opportunities

Through today, the CE administration ensures faculty can avail themselves of the wide array of teacher education opportunities at DLIFLC that are critical to the Institute's initiative to increase graduation requirements. Below, a listing:

- Faculty, Team Leaders, and Administration:
  - Advanced Language Academies. The academies, which are open to other US government language schools and Foreign Language Flagship Programs, afford academic leaders, academic specialists, teacher educators, and faculty the opportunity to discuss the theory and practice of TLLT. Typical topics were Overview of SLA Theories; OACD; Task-Based Instruction; Content-Based Instruction; Learner-Centered Instruction; Formative and Summative Assessments; Genre and Authentic Materials.
  - Summits. Summits focused on a particular topic, such as "Actualizing Open Architecture Curricular Design" (May, 2016), are organized several times per year.
  - 1-Day Language Learning Conferences. Twice yearly, the Faculty Development Division of DLIFLC holds one-day language learning conferences with 25 faculty presenting on topics of interest to professionals. The process for selecting presenters includes blind-review of the proposals.
- Teachers: Teacher Education Series are routinely organized by the Provost Office, e.g., "Reaching 2+: Sharing Successes" occurred every

month for one year. At these sessions, faculty from across DLIFLC described the record-breaking results achieved in their courses.

- Team Leaders: Workshops aimed at the approximately 75 Team Leaders on the main campus are held about subjects such as "Implementating OACD."
- Administration: Workshops take place, e.g., four sessions where participants co-created and presented on "Actions Plans for Reaching Higher Levels of Proficiency."

Learner Education

Learners accustomed to traditional, teacher-centered language learning contexts can be disconcerted when first presented with learner-centered instruction because they have limited experience taking responsibility for their learning, practicing autonomy while accessing learning opportunities 24/7, engaging in collaborative learning situations where they work in pairs and group work, and more. CE teachers offer learners an orientation that helps learners with the transition from teacher-centered to learner-centered instruction. Language learning style and strategy instruction for learners, which is fundamental for making the critical leap from Level 3/Professional to Level 4/Distinguished, follows the orientation. Below, measures taken to reconceptualize learner education in CE:

Provide Learning Style and Strategy Instruction

CE faculty introduce learners to learning style and strategy instruction when they start their courses. Learners are administered a battery of instruments designed to provide information on learning style, which Leaver posits is the "most significant" individual difference related to language learning (2003, p. 53). This battery consists of (1) *E&L Cognitive Styles Construct* (Ehrman & Leaver, 1997, 2002, 2003) for cognitive style; (2) *Myers-Briggs Type Indicator* (*MBTI*) (Myers & Myers, 1980) for personality type; and *Barsch Learning Styles Preference Form* (Barsch, 2003) for sensory preferences. Data gathered from the different instruments is included in an Individualized Study Plan (ISP), providing insights into learner style and which learning strategies can be especially beneficial.

When conducting learning strategy instruction, Oxford's (1990, 2016) classic taxonomy of metacognitive, cognitive, social, and affective learning strategies is the preferred guide. Shekhtman (2003a, 2003b, 2003c, Shekhtman et al, 2002) adds communication strategies as a category, asserting they are especially important at the higher levels.

Leaver and Shekhtman (2002) posit that the nature of learning strategies necessarily changes according to proficiency level. For example, strategies for comprehending authentic printed texts such as guessing from context, using titles and visuals appearing with the RC text or LC passage as clues, circumlocution, use of cognates clues, and such are helpful at the lower levels. Risk-taking applies to all levels. Below, some examples of learning strategies for high-level learners recommended by Leaver (2003):

- Metacognitive: Planning study activities; practicing advance organization; observing learning effectiveness; evaluating progress; rewarding progress; and revising plans.

- Cognitive: Memorizing/associating; compensating (rarely needed); processing (recycling, manipulation for practice, use of synonymy, and "-lect" switching, which is understanding the differences among sociolects, dialects, and idiolects).

- Social: Asking a native to proof written text or listen to a speech; reviewing movies and books with native speaker friends and colleagues; asking a native-speaker mentor to help with the development of cognitive strategies.

- Affective: Practicing positive self-talk after hearing criticism from native speakers about a linguistic mistake or socio-linguistic misstep; keeping a journal.

- Communication: for LC—Using the interlocutor, managing the input; for RC—comparing genres, using topic saturation, and comparing interpretations; For SP—developing and using automatic discourse, using authentic materials, using conversational repair, embellishing speech, and controlling the conversation; Writing—developing and using automatic discourse, using authentic materials, using process writing, embellishing, and obtaining authentic feedback.

Use Individualized Study Plans (ISP)

An ISP referred to briefly earlier, is a key tool in the arsenal of the learner dedicated to reaching Levels 3+ and beyond. According to Leaver (2003b), the purpose of an ISP is "to assist students in organizing their short-term and long-term learning goals and activities" (p. v). The *ISP*, which all learners in CE work with their teachers to construct, reflects the learning objectives, learning experiences, interests, learning style, and financial/time constraints of the learner. Although no specific format is required, most *ISPs* include "courses; study, work and travel abroad; independent study; reading; use of the Internet; work with a native speaker; development of friendships with speakers of the language; writing to pen-pals (and/

or friends and relatives); practica and internships; watching television; listening to the radio and tapes; becoming acquainted with music, arts, and dance; foreign assignments; and periodical assessment of progress" (Leaver, 2003b, p. 4). Included is important information about learning style and learning strategies, which were discussed in the preceding section.

The data can be organized accordingly:

- Skill-based plans (LC, RC, SP, and Writing [WR]);
- topic-based plans (specialized and general, based on, for example, work needs or future plans for the language);
- proficiency-based plans (development of discourse, linguistic, sociolinguistic, strategic, and socio-cultural competence);
- and chronological plans.

Set up a Diagnostic and Dynamic Assessment Program

Dynamic Assessment (DA), which was briefly examined in the "Curricular Design" section above, and Diagnostic Assessment[48] are both valuable learning tools focused on learner improvement. Currently, DLIFLC is implementing both. Diagnostic Assessment is a formative learning tool created at DLIFLC in 1996 to diagnose learner strengths and weaknesses in the four skills of LC, RC, SP, and Writing (WR) (Steven Koppany, cited in Cohen, 2003). It both identifies problem areas in the four skills and provides clear recommendations for how the learner can improve performance. Linguistic breakdown is a focal point because it provides critical information to the assessor about learner problem areas.

Diagnostic Assessment consists of a three-skill interview in LC, RC, and SP with two assessors and a learner that lasts 90 minutes, although it can be extended according to learner needs. Thirty minutes are allotted to assess each skill. Diagnostic Assessment begins with the SP component—an oral interview based on the ILR OPI that establishes the learner's current proficiency level in SP and serves to familiarize the learner with the process. One assessor engages with the learner, clarifying that Diagnostic Assessment is not a test but a way to help the learner remedy problem areas. The other assessor takes notes about learner performance. Concrete recommendations for dealing with the problem areas are prepared by the assessor and delivered to the learner in a *Learning Plan*, which complements the *ISP* described earlier.

In the RC portion, the learner is presented with at least three texts—one at the learner's proficiency level, as indicated by performance in the SP part, one at a bit higher level, and one at a much higher level. The learner reads silently and then dis-

---

48   Given the acronym for Diagnostic Assessment is identical to that of Dynamic Assessment, the former will be referred to by its full name.

cusses its main idea and details, in either the target language (TL) or English, with the assessor. Given the goal is to assess RC, not SP, use of the TL is not required although learners at Level 3 and above generally prefer the TL to English. The assessor asks the learner pointed questions to determine levels of understanding.

The LC part can assess either interactive and non-interactive LC or both, depending on institutional needs. In the former, one assessor simultaneously evaluates SP and LC. Cohen (2003) suggests an alternative—lengthen the interview to focus on SP in the first part and LC in the second part. Concerning non-interactive LC, the learner is asked to listen to passages, which can be replayed so memory is not a confounding variable. As with RC, given the goal is to assess LC, not SP, use of the TL is not required, although learners at Level 3 and above generally prefer the TL to English. The assessor asks the learner pointed questions to determine levels of understanding.

Cohen (2003) asserts that "[a] Diagnostic Assessment is especially advantageous for higher level language learners" because "[e]specially at L3, students do not know what their gaps are" (p. 29).

Promote Learner Voice

Learners grasped soon after arriving in CE that they were an essential part of the community of participants cited earlier. The OACD principle—Ongoing learner involvement in the selection and delivery of content, requires learners lean forward and take responsibility for their learning throughout the course. Sensing Sessions are opportunities for learners to provide weekly, monthly, bi-monthly or quarterly feedback to a teacher(s) and/or administrator(s) about aspects of the academic program such as the teachers, curriculum, use of technology and more. The feedback, which is uncensored but respectful in tone, is an important source of information to teacher(s) and/or administrator(s) which can be used to improve processes. The person in charge of the Sensing Session, who can be the teacher of the learners, another teacher, a department chairperson, a Dean, etc., arrives with a laptop or flipchart to take notes. The person alerts the learners at the start that it is critical to (a) be fair and honest; (b) be respectful when providing constructive criticism; (c) not project personal frustrations unrelated to learning against the teacher(s) and/or administrator(s); and (d) be cognizant of the power they have when asked for their opinion in this type of forum. The learners are told they can comment as often as they wish, first citing the positive aspects, then the areas of concern. At the end, the person in charge asks the learners to vote in order to identify what areas of concern might be shared by the majority. These areas are then communicated to the other teachers in the case of team teaching. The feedback to the teacher(s) is formative, not summative, i.e. the feedback is not used by the administrator(s) to evaluate the teacher(s); rather it is used as a tool for professional development. The teacher or teaching team then systematically works to correct the areas of concern. Sensing Sessions are an efficient way to enhance inter- and intra-group communication.

Defense Threat Reduction Agency Program

The Defense Threat Reduction Agency (DTRA) Interpreting Course in Russian at DLIFLC is an intensive program for learners of Russian whose assignments within the government require a high level of language proficiency for conducting weapons control work in Russia. Thirteen faculty are dedicated to achieving the goals of Levels 3+ and above in LC and RC, and Level 3 and above in SP. Starting in February 2020, DTRA learners who meet graduation requirements will receive 87 college credits, the majority 300 to 400 level courses, as per the American Council on Education (ACE).

When creating the curriculum, teachers apply principles of OACD. The theme-based syllabi covering 24 general topic areas such as history, economics, political science, technology, and health, and specific topic areas such as the latest developments in foreign policy is negotiated with learners. Teachers, working with learners, create daily assignments based on current authentic materials that are previewed before class, following the flipped classroom approach. Teachers also develop new courses based on trend analyses across and within groups of graduating learners. For example, to help learners develop greater register range, DTRA teachers designed a Stylistics Course that highlights the distinctive styles found in various literary and nonliterary genres and in the works of individual writers. Below, the themes examined in the Stylistics Course:

The notion of norm and variability in language use. Standard and colloquial styles. Word order and sentence structure: comparative typology of the Russian and English languages.
Classification of functional styles of the Russian language. Description of linguistic means, sub-styles and speech genres typical of each style in the Russian language.
Emotional and expressive aspects of the language. Expressive suffixes in the Russian language. Tropes: similes, types of metaphors, irony, hyperboles, litotes.
Types of phraseological units: set phrases, idioms, proverbs and sayings, their role in stylistics. Challenges for interpreters.

Teachers, acting as mentors/coaches/advisors, continually urge learners to use higher-order thinking skills as they research topics for roundtables and presentations. A formal roundtable discussion on a controversial topic takes place every two weeks. Learners study the topic in depth to be ready to discuss it in detail. One of the learners acts as moderator and organizes the discussion by preparing three to four thought-provoking questions.

In addition to roundtable discussions, learners also make frequent 10–15-minute presentations on topics they have researched. The presentations are followed by elaboration activities such as debates, which encourage analysis, synthesis, evaluation (and later, creativity) as per Bloom's (1956) taxonomy of learning objectives. Learners have ample time to prepare for debates, working collaboratively in teams. One instructor works with each team separately. All instructors act as judges, although in one debate more advanced learners in the same program are judges. Teachers direct learners to relevant websites, provide higher-level, register-appropriate expressions and connectors, and review learners' work before it is presented. To develop greater accuracy in the target language, learners attend required grammar sessions and individualized speaking sessions with teachers, where they review the fossilized errors detected by teachers during the activities.

In the DTRA course, learners take interpreting excursions to local sites, though this activity has been curtailed because of the pandemic. Examples of sites are: Community Hospital of the Monterey Peninsula, the USS Hornet, the local Police Station, US Coast Guard Station, Colton Hall Museum, Monterey Bay Aquarium, Monterey Airport, and Naval Postgraduate School Laboratories. Pairs in the class of six prepare a 10-15 mt. presentation in Russian about some aspect of the site to be visited. Learner A gives the presentation; Learner B engages in simultaneous, consecutive interpreting into English. Learners have two weeks to prepare for the interpreting excursion. The real-life activities help prepare learners for their future work. Due to the number of interpreting excursions from eight to 16.

Another activity is the in-class mini-excursion where Learner A gives a detailed briefing to peers in Russian while Learner B interprets into English (and vice versa). Both briefers and the audience are expected to ask questions, making the experience interactive. Interpreting for guest speakers, who make interactive presentations lasting up to two hours, is a challenge for learners who are about to graduate.

In addition to the activities listed, DTRA learners engage in two-hour negotiation scenarios, where they are immersed in a variety of contexts, e.g., discussion between union officials and company representatives about salary and benefits, etc. Learners receive critiques on their performance from both teachers and peers.

Over the years, the results in LC, RC, and SP in the DTRA Interpreting Courses have continually risen due, in great part, to the program improvements outlined earlier. In 2017, 35% achieved Levels 3+ and 4 in at least one of the three skills; 2018, 46%; 2019, 49%; 2020, 63%. (More specific information is inaccessible.)

Conclusion

Reconceptualizing language programs with the goal of Level 3+ and above is a complex enterprise that presents challenges in the areas of curricular design, teacher education, and learner education. Examining frameworks that have consistently produced high levels of proficiency can provide ideas for improving learner performance. While some might question the generalizability of some of the principles and activities in the CE framework to the K-16 environment, the basic concepts are directly applicable to learners aged 16 and above.

While every learning context is *sui generis*, a veritable universe onto itself, given the interplay of myriad variables in the areas of human resources, materials, and fiscal resources, measures that apply to most contexts do exist that can be systematically applied to increase the probability for success. This chapter has presented a sampling of measures for the purposes of reflection and possible adoption.

References

American Council on the Teaching of Foreign Languages. (2018). *Testing Workshop*. Interagency Language Roundtable. Washington, DC. Council on the Teaching of Foreign Languages, Alexandria, VA.

Arce, J. (2000). Developing voices: Transformative education in a first-grade two-way Spanish immersion classroom: A participatory study. *Bilingual Research Journal*, 24(3), 249–260.

Bailey, K., & Freeman, D. (1990). *Creating a community of understanding; creating a community of practice.* Defense Language Institute Foreign Language Center Faculty Development Workshop. Presidio of Monterey, CA.

Bachman, L. (1990). *Fundamental considerations in language testing.* Oxford: Oxford University Press.

Barsch, J. (2003). *Barsch Learning Style Preference Form*. Texas Center for Adult Literacy. Downloaded from http://www-tcall.tamu.edu/research/NSO/LS/LS_a.htm.

Bloom, B. (Ed.). (1956). *Taxonomy of educational objectives, Handbook I: Cognitive domain*. New York: David McKay.

Campbell, C. (2020). Open architecture curricular design: A fundamental principle of transformative language learning and teaching." In B. L. Leaver, D. Davidson, and C. Campbell (Eds.), *Transformative language learning and teaching* (pp. 43-50). Cambridge, UK: Cambridge University Press.

Campbell, C., & Sarac, B. (2017). The role of technology in language learning in the twenty-first century: Perspectives from academe, government, and the private sector. *Hispania*, 100(5, Centenary Issue): 77–84.

Clifford, R. T. (1988). What you test is what you get: Open versus closed instructional systems. *Die Unterrichtspraxis* 21(1): 37–40.

Cohen, B. (2003). *Diagnostic assessment at the superior-Distinguished threshold.* Salinas, CA: MSI Press.

Cohen, B. (2015). *Enhanced final learning objectives activities.* Faculty Presentations at the Defense Language Institute Foreign Language Center. Presidio of Monterey, CA.

Corin, A. (2020). The challenge of the inverted pyramid in attaining Distinguished-level proficiency. *Journal for Distinguished Language Studies* 7: 85-114..

Dababneh, R., & Yuan, R. (2020. accepted for publication). Applications of formative and dynamic assessment in the school of resident education, DLIFLC. In A. Corin, B. L. Leaver, & C. Campbell (Eds.), *Open Architecture Curricular Design: Concepts and courses.* Publisher TBD.

Davidson, D., & Garas, N. (2018). *360 survey.* Unpublished report for the Flagship Culture Initiative.

Davidson, D., & Shaw, J. (2019). A cross-linguistic and cross-skill perspective on L2 development in study abroad. In P. Winke & S. Gass (Eds.), *Foreign language proficiency in higher education* (pp. 217–242). Cham, Switzerland: Springer.

Duri, J. (1992). Content-based instruction: Keeping DLI on the cutting edge. *The Globe* 5: 4-5.

Ehrman, M. (2002). Understanding the learner at the superior-Distinguished threshold. In B. L. Leaver & B. Shekhtman. (Eds.), *Developing professional-level language proficiency* (pp.245-259). Cambridge, UK: Cambridge University Press.

Erhman, M. & Leaver, B. L. (1997). *Sorting out global and analytic functions in second language learning.* American Association of Applied Linguistics Annual Meeting. Orlando, FL.

Ehrman, M., & Leaver, B. L. (2002). *The E&L Cognitive Styles Construct.* Unpublished, copyrighted manuscript.

Ehrman, M., & Leaver, B. L. (2003). Cognitive styles in the service of language learning. *System* 31(3): 393-415.

Farraj, A. (2006). Raising the bar: E-learning for obtaining the Distinguished level in the Arabic language. *Journal for Distinguished Language Studies* 4: 21-30.

Foster, E. (1997). Transformative learning in adult second language learning. *New Directions for Adult and Continuing Education* 74: 33 - 40.

Franke, J. (2020). *Pursuing Distinguished speaking proficiency with adult foreign language learners: A case study.* Unpublished doctoral dissertation. Indianapolis, IN: American College of Education.

Goulah, J. (2006). Transformative second and foreign language learning for the 21st century. *Critical Inquiry in Language Studies: An International Journal* 3(4): 201–221.

Ingold, C. (2002). The LangNet "Reading to the Four" Project: Applied Technology at Higher Levels of Language Learning." In B. L. Leaver & B. Shekhtman (Eds.). *Developing professional-level language proficiency* (pp. 141-155). Cambridge, UK: Cambridge University Press.

Leaver, B. L. (1989). Dismantling classroom walls for increased foreign language proficiency. *Foreign Language Annals* 22(1): 67-74.

Leaver, B. L. (2003a). *Achieving native-like second language proficiency: A catalogue of critical factors.* Salinas, CA: MSI Press.

Leaver, B. L. (2003b). *Individualized study plans for very advanced students of foreign languages.* Salinas, CA: MSI Press.

Leaver, B. L. (2020). Transformative language learning and teaching: The next paradigm shift and its historical context. In B. L. Leaver, D. Davidson, & C. Campbell, C. (Eds.), *Transformative language learning and teaching* (pp. 13-22). Cambridge, UK: Cambridge University Press.

Leaver, B.L. & Atwell, S. (2002). Preliminary qualitative findings from a study of the processes leading to the advanced professional proficiency level (ILR 4). B. L. Leaver & B. S. Shekhtman (Eds.), *Developing professional-level language proficiency* (pp. 260-279). Cambridge, UK: Cambridge University Press.

Leaver, B. L. & Campbell, C. (2015). "Experience with higher levels of proficiency." In T. Brown & J. Bown (Eds.), *To advanced proficiency and beyond: Theory and methods for developing superior second-language ability* (pp. 3–22). Washington, DC: Georgetown University Press.

Leaver, B. L., & Campbell, C. (2020). The shifting paradigm in Russian language programs from communicative language teaching to transformative language learning and teaching. In E. Dengub, I. Dubinina, & J. Merrill (Eds.). *Art of teaching Russian.* Washington, DC: Georgetown University Press.

Leaver, B. L., Campbell, C., Nyikos, M., & Oxford, R. L. (2019). "Transforming the transformers: Breaking through philosophical, cognitive, and emotional barriers. Society, Identity, and Transformation in Language Teacher Education Conference. Minneapolis, MN.

Leaver, B. L., Davidson, D., & Campbell, C. (Eds.). (2020). *Transformative Language Learning and Teaching.* Cambridge, UK: Cambridge University Press.

Leaver, B. L. & Granoien, N. (2000). Философия образования: Почему мы преподаем определенными путями. [Philosophy of education: Why we teach the way we do]. *Философия Образования* [Philosophy of Education] 1(1): 3–9.

Leaver, B. L,. & Shekhtman, B. (Eds.). (2002). *Developing professional-level language proficiency*. Cambridge, UK: Cambridge University Press.

Mezirow, J., & Associates. (Eds.). (2000). *Learning as transformation: Critical perspectives on a theory in progress*. San Francisco: Jossey-Bass.

McClinton, J. (2005). Transformative learning: The English as a second language teacher's experience. *The CATESOL Journal* 17(1): 156–163.

Myers, I. Briggs, with Myers, Peter. (1980). *Gifts differing*. Palo Alto, CA: Consulting Psychologists.

Osterling, J., & Webb, W. (2009). On becoming a bilingual teacher: A transformative process for preservice and novice teachers. *Journal of Transformative Education* 7(4): 267–293.

Oxford, R. (1990). *Language learning strategies: What every teacher should know*. New York: Newbury House Publishers.

Oxford, R. (2016). *Teaching and researching language learning strategies*. London: Routledge.

Poehner, M., & Lantolf, J. (2003). Dynamic assessment of l2 development: Bringing the past into the future. *CALPER Working Papers, No. 1* (October). University Park, PA: Center for Advanced Language Proficiency Education and Research, The Pennsylvania State University.

Poehner, M., & Lantolf, J. (2005). Dynamic assessment in the language classroom. *Language Teaching Research* 9(3): 233-265.

Poehner, M., Davin, K., & Lantolf, J. (2017). Dynamic assessment. In E. Shohamy, I. Or, & S. May (Eds.). *Language testing and assessment. Encyclopedia of Language and Education* (3rd ed.). Cham, Switzerland: Springer.

Robin, R. (2008). Distinguished speakers and screen-time repertoire. *Journal for Distinguished Language Studies* 5: 7-10.

Sandrock, P. (2010). *The keys to assessing language performance: A teacher's manual for measuring student progress*. Alexandria, VA: The American Council on the Teaching of Foreign Languages.

Shekhtman, B. (2003a). Do superior-level students need language instruction? An essay in answer to the myth of natural acquisition and self-study being sufficient at high levels of foreign language acquisition. *ACTR Newsletter* 30(2), 1-3.

Shekhtman. B. (2003b). *How to improve your foreign language IMMEDIATELY*. Salinas, CA: MSI Press.

Shekhtman, B. (2003c). *Working with advanced foreign language students*. Salinas, CA: MSI Press.

Shekhtman, B., Leaver, B. L., with N. Lord, E. Kuznetsova, & E. Ovtcharenko. (2002). Developing professional-level oral proficiency: The Shekhtman method of communicative teaching. In B. L. Leaver & B. Shekhtman (Eds.), *Developing professional-level language proficiency* (pp. 119-140). Cambridge, UK: Cambridge University Press.

Soudakoff, S. (2004). Developing 3+/4 Reading and Translation Skills for Presidential Needs: A Summary. *Journal for Distinguished Language Studies* 2: 19-22.

Spence-Brown, R. (2003). Authentic assessment? The implementation of an "Authentic" Teaching and Assessment Task. Unpublished doctoral dissertation. Melbourne, Australia: University of Melbourne.

The National Standards Collaborative Board. (2019). *World-Readiness standards for learning languages* (4th ed.). Downloaded from www.actfl.org/sites/default/files/publications/standards/World-ReadinessStandardsforLearningLa nguages.pdf.

Wiggins, G. (1998). *Educative assessment: Designing assessments to inform and improve student performance.* San Francisco, CA: Jossey-Bass.

To Superior and Beyond: Developing Professional Proficiency in a Fourth-Year Russian Program

Tony Brown, Jennifer Bown, Katya Jordan, & Elizaveta Kurganova

Abstract

A growing number of specialists in the field of ESL/EFL are beginning to incorporate the long-established tradition of debate into the foreign language classroom as a way of achieving high levels of proficiency. Such an approach has proven beneficial to the development of critical thinking and general speaking, reading, listening, and writing skills. This article addresses a number of scaffolded pedagogical techniques employed in two consecutive fourth-year Russian-language courses, the first of which (Russian 421) employs current events as the *modus operandi* for teaching presentational speech in preparation for the second course (Russian 422) that operationalizes presentational speech in the culminating rhetorical exercise of debate. A thorough description of the major tasks is provided, which for Russian 421 include weekly extensive listening assignments and three research projects that culminate in in-class presentations, whereas for Russian 422—intensive reading, role plays, and debates. The article likewise addresses the objective of internships in the fourth-year Russian curriculum and includes a discussion of how time in country coupled with level-appropriate language instruction accelerate proficiency gain at all levels. A curriculum that aligns learning tasks with desired proficiency outcomes and that provides scaffolding to complete those tasks both in the classroom and in a professional setting serves to bridge formal language instruction with real-world application and contribute to life-long learning.

Keywords: Russian language, debate, language proficiency, professional,

curriculum.

The fourth-year curriculum at Brigham Young University (BYU) focuses on moving students beyond the Advanced-level[49] of proficiency as they develop skills in presentational writing, speaking, and debate. The two-course sequence aims not only to facilitate development of language proficiency but also to help students acquire important twenty-first-century skills and to become lifelong learners. An important ancillary to the fourth-year curriculum is the professional internship program in Moscow, Russia and Riga, Latvia.

In this paper, we will provide information about the fourth-year curriculum, detailing the instructional approach and assignments that facilitate development of higher-level proficiency.

Literature Review

Many universities in the United States and other countries offer courses in argumentation and debate with the dual objective of teaching rhetorical skills and improving students' command of their first language, but such courses have not been common in L2 curricula. Collaborative learning in the form of oral debate mirrors what Swain (1993) refers to as the output hypothesis, in that students "push their linguistic competence to its limit as they attempt to express their ideas" (p. 162) and as they negotiate meaning. In discussing the function of rhetoric, Inch and Warnick (2005) point out that "we use language that enables us to achieve the particular outcome we seek" (p. 112). Ultimately, according to these two authors, "the rhetorical function of language aims to direct or influence thoughts and behavior. It is persuasive" (Ibid.). Shekhtman et al. (2003) point out that aspiring Level 4 students gravitate to debate and related tasks because such tasks "contribute toward building 4-level speaking competency and because they directly satisfy professional needs" (p. 32).

The long-established tradition of using debate as an instructional technique in content classes across the sciences and humanities has proven beneficial to the development of critical thinking and general communication skills (Elliot, 1993; Musselman, 2004; Osborne, 2005; Roy & Macchiette, 2005; Vo & Morris, 2006; Zare & Othman, 2015). The use of debate in the EFL/ESL classroom is not a novel approach, either (Cornway, 1976; Stokes, 1976), and has been shown to improve English-speaking skills (Aclan & Aziz, 2015; Fauzan, 2016; Tavakoli et al., 2017).

Research conducted by Massie (2005) and Connor (1987) identifies the task of debate as a valuable strategy in improving L2 oral and written proficiency, particularly at the Advanced level and beyond. Supporting and defending opinions is a core task at the higher proficiency levels, and the criteria outlined in the ACTFL

---

49   In this paper, we use "Advanced" to describe a particular level on the American Council on the Teaching of Foreign Languages proficiency scale, while we use "advanced" to refer to more generic descriptions of courses or topics.

speaking performance profile dovetail with qualities emphasized in public speaking and debate, i.e., pronunciation, fluency, breadth of vocabulary, sociolinguistic/cultural appropriateness, grammatical accuracy, and debate-related communicative tasks.

Pronunciation

The forum of debate lends itself to an acquisition-rich environment in which students exchange competing views that necessitate a level of pronunciation that does not detract from the message. Morley (2005) dismisses "yesterday's goals of 'perfect' pronunciation and 'near-native' pronunciation" as "patently unattainable" and, instead, emphasizes "helping students achieve improved intelligibility as an overall target" (p. 9). Such an observation properly weights the relative importance of pronunciation (as evidenced by its appearance in the ACTFL Guidelines only at the Distinguished level). Instructors play an essential role in developing this and other language skills by helping their students learn how to learn. Indeed, students "need guidance in developing speech awareness, personal speech-monitoring skills, and speech modification strategies, which will enable them to continue to enhance their intelligibility, communicability, and confidence outside class, as well as inside" (Ibid., p. 10).

Fluency

Fluency of speech characterizes an experienced public speaker. Similarly, high-level speakers of a foreign language easily connect thoughts, thus moving beyond sentential level speech to that of connected, cohesive paragraphs, and even "highly sophisticated and tightly organized extended discourse" (ACTFL Proficiency Guidelines – Speaking, 2012), such as that required in oral presentations and debates

Vocabulary

Redding (1954) asserts that "although it should be obvious that argumentative discourse requires extraordinary precision in vocabulary, many debaters have been known to toss about, with gleeful abandon, vague and ambiguous terms. The debater, like any public speaker, should command a precision of word choice that will reflect the most subtle shadings of meaning" (p. 205). Shekhtman et al. (2003) likewise argues that presentational speech "helps the student acquire the necessary professional vocabulary by providing a context for it" (p. 33). In short, breadth of vocabulary facilitates accuracy by sharpening one's precision of meaning and fluency and expanding one's capacity to provide uninterrupted, extended, in-depth discourse on a topic, rather than spotty, fragmented statements that lack transitions, cohesion, and continuity.

Sociolinguistic/Cultural Appropriateness

Argumentation challenges one's ability to demonstrate intellectual prowess, cultural sophistication, and wittiness. As such, manner of presentation, in the form of idiomatic statements and reference to cultural artifacts, plays an important role in determining the outcome of a debate. Indeed, failure to express oneself in a culturally appropriate manner potentially can stifle communication more than linguistic mistakes would.

Similarly, high-level speakers distinguish themselves in their ability to make cultural references to the target language culture and control the range of registers needed to respond appropriately in professional situations and in conversational settings using colloquial language. In fact, Shekhtman et al. (2003) contend that "[t]ailoring language to the audience is one of the more salient attributes that distinguishes a Level 4 language user from a Level 3 language user" (p. 40).

Grammatical Accuracy

Correct usage of grammar naturally plays an important role in any public discourse, including public speaking. Sentence construction in oral presentation tends to have a looser structure than in most forms of writing, but certainly not at the expense of grammatical rules. Level 3 and Level 4 speakers may make occasional grammatical errors, but such errors do not reflect a recurring pattern.

Communicative Tasks

Shekhtman et al. (2003) highlight seven tasks that Level 4 professional language users should be able to accomplish "in much the same way as an educated native speaker, without resorting to compensation strategies and with the same effectiveness" (p. 31), in particular: 1) problem-solving discussion (situation); 2) informally interpreting language and culture; 3) interview; 4) briefing; 5) formal presentation; 6) debate; and 7) negotiation. Indeed, according to the aforementioned authors, "The ability of a student to participate actively and successfully in a professional argument in the target language attests to almost native-like proficiency and is listed in the FILR [Federal Interagency Language Roundtable] Proficiency Descriptors (1999) as one of the attributes of Level 4 proficiency" (Ibid., p. 34).

The potential benefits of using debate in a foreign language classroom go beyond oral proficiency gains; debate appears to work well as a strategy to build written argumentative skills, i.e., the skill of writing an argumentative essay, which, in turn, can be utilized in content-based courses. Content-based methods set out to imbue language with authenticity such that language becomes the vehicle for communicating ideas for meaningful purposes rather than functioning solely as an object of study (Freels et al., 2017; Frodesen & Holten, 2003; Hartwell, 1985; Hedegaard, 2005; Jourdenais & Shaw, 2005; Long, 2007; MLA Ad Hoc Committee,

2007; Shaw, 1997; Stryker & Leaver, 1997; van Lier, 2005)—an educational philosophy that describes what Leaver and Shekhtman term "transactional," or "developing problem-solving skills" (2002, p. 4). Such a philosophy speaks to a preference in US instruction, including foreign language classrooms, and comprises the framework not only for content-based learning but also for task-based, problem-based, and project-based learning—all of which contribute to the forum of debate.

A growing number of specialists in the field of ESL/EFL are beginning to incorporate debate practices into the foreign language classroom as a way of achieving proficiency gain at the Advanced level. In November 2011, Paulina De Santis of the Defense Language Institute presented at the annual American Council on the Teaching of Foreign Languages (ACTFL) conference on "The Power of Debate in L2 Learning." Preliminary findings examining the value of such an approach overwhelmingly affirm the effectiveness of debate (Brown, 2012; Brown et al., 2009; Brown et al., 2011); however, attaining high levels of proficiency requires intensive scaffolded learning and training, both at home and abroad.

Indeed, mere exposure to and study of advanced-level curricular materials, such as literary works and journal articles in the target language, do not by any means ensure uptake (cf. Donato & Brooks, 2004) any more than mere exposure to the language while living in the target language culture ensures uptake (cf. Davidson, 2002); however, time in country coupled with level-appropriate language instruction offer depth and breadth of input and consistent corrective feedback—the combination of which accelerates proficiency gain at all levels. To dismiss the element of formal language instruction in the context of working in the target language environment is to underestimate the role of the instructor in detecting and correcting otherwise fossilized forms, which can occur even at the Superior level (Ehrman, 2002a, 2002b). As Shekhtman (2005) writes in this regard, "It is true that it is easier for Superior-level language students to improve their language on their own, independently, without an instructor, especially when they live in the target country, but it is also true that professional language instruction makes this improvement more effective, efficient, and rapid. Language instruction helps students to diagnose their language level, define their strengths and weaknesses, and enrich their language with more sophisticated grammar structures and refined vocabulary. The most important effect of language instruction, however, lies in the increasing level of automaticity" (p. 71).

Successful implementation of debate in the classroom requires thoughtful and attentive scaffolding. Students who already have attained oral proficiency levels of Advanced-High and beyond, knowingly or not, bring with them incorrect fossilized forms that require unlearning so as to avoid building on an already compromised foundation (cf. Brown et al., 2011). The consequences of hastily bypassing the difficult process of training may not be felt in terms of sheer production, but certainly will manifest themselves in inaccuracies. Past research suggests that neglecting accuracy, particularly during the formative stages of language learning, can have detrimental effects on students' ability to monitor and to maintain a balance between functional competence and grammatical accuracy at the professional level and beyond (Brecht et al., 1993; Higgs & Clifford, 1982). Wolfe-Quintero et al. (1998, p. 33) insightfully point out that "in second language learning, if the representation is faulty but access is fully automatized, it may lead to production that is error-full but impervious to change (perhaps the source of what has been called fossilization)."

Conversely, research suggests that those who make the requisite effort to defossilize incorrect grammatical forms eventually surpass in proficiency those who activize an ever-expanding lexicon using error-ridden constructions (Brown, et al., 2011). Shekhtman et al. (2003) discuss a number of potential discourse devices designed to prepare students for debate, which they designate as "complication exercises," defined as exercises that "help students raise their proficiency to a higher level, enrich their speech with more sophisticated patterns, and, for this reason, can be considered the most important tactic for Superior-level students" (Ibid., p. 34). Moreover, the authors argue that such exercises are "based on the language instructor's analysis of students' speech and consequent introduction of speech improvements, which students then automate. This kind of exercise is critical for developing students' skill in preparing papers and oral presentations of professional topics" (Ibid., pp. 34-35). To this end, the authors propose a series of exercises designed to build linguistic and sociolinguistic competence (see Shekhtman et al. 2003 for a complete list of suggested exercises).

Accordingly, this article will put forward a number of scaffolded pedagogical techniques employed in two consecutive fourth-year Russian-language courses, the first of which employs current events as the modus operandi for teaching presentational speech in preparation for the second course that operationalizes presentational speech in the culminating rhetorical exercise of debate.

The Fourth-Year Curriculum

The fourth-year curriculum at BYU consists of two literature courses (Russian 441, nineteenth-century literature, and Russian 442, twentieth-century literature) conducted entirely in the target language, as well as two advanced language courses, Russian 421 and 422, which are focused on proficiency in all four skills, with a particular focus on developing presentational writing and speaking skills. In addition, fourth-year students are encouraged to complete a Russian-speaking internship either in Moscow Russia or in Riga, Latvia. The internship, however, is not a requirement to earn a major in Russian and, as a result, students complete the internship at their own convenience—sometimes in the third year, sometimes in the summer. During the internship program, students can earn credit for either

Russian 421 or Russian 422. The internship experience will be described in greater detail later.

Although Russian 421 and 422 are independent courses, both instructors have worked together to ensure a smooth transition between courses, as well as a focus on moving students towards Superior-level proficiency. Russian 421 focuses primarily on listening and presentational speaking, while Russian 422 puts a stronger emphasis on reading and interpersonal speaking in the form of debates. Both courses focus on developing 1) appropriateness of expression, 2) precision of lexicon, 3) discourse competence, and 4) linguistic sophistication and accuracy—which are the primary needs that Leaver and Shekhtman (2002) identify for learners at the threshold between ILR 2 and 3. In addition, both courses seek to promote the development of learner autonomy, as well as such skills as communication; critical thinking and problem solving; information, media and technology literacy; social and cross-cultural skills; and productivity and accountability (21st Century Skills Map—World Languages, 2011).

Russian 421 focuses on Russia's current events and uses listening and reading materials available online through Russian-language news outlets; for this reason, the course does not use a textbook. While some of the materials, especially those pertaining to information literacy and the practice of journalism, are prepared by the instructor, the students act as co-creators of the course as they select materials for their research projects and as they share these materials with their peers. Furthermore, a significant emphasis is placed on metacognition.

Russian 422, by contrast, makes use of the textbook Mastering Russian Through Global Debate (Brown, Balykhina, Talalakina, Bown, & Kurilenko, 2014). Topics from the textbook drive course content and students engage in intensive reading of texts, as well as work on vocabulary and grammatical structures found therein. In addition, the textbook is supplemented by media and activities.

The primary goals of the two-course sequence include the following:
1. Expand vocabulary, improve phrase development skills, and learn to create more complex text types;
2. Improve ability to state and support informed opinions and organize arguments;
3. Foster ability to hypothesize in Russian;
4. Use intensive reading as a method for learning vocabulary, understanding text structure, and improving language (within familiar and unfamiliar topics); and
5. Use extensive listening as a method for increasing understanding of information presented in most genres (on familiar and unfamiliar topics).

The two courses also have secondary objectives, focused on the development of twenty-first-century skills as articulated by the Partnership for 21st Century Skills (2011). These skills include Communication; Critical Thinking and Problem Solving; Information, Media, and Technology Literacy; Social and Cross-Cultural Skills; and Productivity and Accountability (21st Century Skills Map—World Languages, 2011).

The major tasks in Russian 421 include weekly extensive listening assignments and three research projects that culminate in in-class presentations, each of which will be described in the following section. The major tasks in Russian 422 include intensive reading, role plays, and debates. In addition, students engage in other support activities that help raise their awareness of linguistic forms and increase their accuracy with more complex lexicon and linguistic structures. Another important component of the fourth-year curriculum concerns self-assessment and goal-setting, important components of metacognition.

Learning Contracts

Self-assessment and goal setting. Although the primary goal of the fourth-year curriculum is to promote development of oral and written proficiency, a secondary goal is development of skills necessary for life-long learning. For most students, Russian 421 and 422 represent their final university language courses. Most will not continue formal study of Russian after graduation; thus, one of the objectives is to help students to evaluate their own learning and develop strategies for life-long learning. Accordingly, during the first week of each course, learners become acquainted with the ACTFL proficiency guidelines and listen to and read samples of language at each level of proficiency. Students use the ACTFL Can-do Statements to ascertain their own abilities in reading, listening, presentational writing, interpersonal speaking, and presentational speaking. Students also submit writing samples and recorded speech samples, as well as engage in a conversation with an instructor trained in OPI testing and rating. The instructor helps guide students' self-assessments and suggests realistic goals for the semester.

As part of setting goals, students are asked to determine evidence by which to measure their improvement. Acceptable evidence includes the reading level of their texts (students are asked to analyze their texts and transcribed speech using readability.io, a free online program that determines the grade level of a text), and their own analysis related to such questions as average sentence length, average number of clauses per sentence, etc. At the end of the semester, students revisit their initial learning contract and the ACTFL Can-Do Statements, record their reflections, and provide evidence of their progress.

Identifying resources and strategies. As part of their learning contracts, students are asked to identify specific resources and strategies that they will use in order to achieve their goals. Early in the semester, students are introduced to new methods for learning vocabulary. Specifically, they learn about the limitations of Google Translate and are introduced to tools such as Linguee, Reverso Context, as well as corpora and concordancers. The instructor then trains them how to use corpora for identifying collocations and how to use search engines as a makeshift corpus for determining appropriate context and usage.

Students contribute to a class wiki where resources for reading and listening can be shared with one another. Favorite websites include Эхо Москвы (Echo of Moscow), idebate.ru, and argumentator.org. Episodes of Дебаты открытого мира (open-world debates) introduce learners to the style of debate used in class, as well as to many of the issues surrounding our debate topics.

Students are directed to choose specific strategies and to keep themselves accountable for their methods. Some students choose to listen to particular podcasts, such as Особое мнение (particular opinion) every night, while others focus on extensive reading or extensive writing. Every three weeks, students submit a written record of their learning efforts.

Extensive Listening

Extensive listening, like extensive reading, involves listening to large quantities of material with the purpose of general comprehension. Extensive listening and reading are important for building proficiency at the Advanced level and beyond, as such activities provide the input necessary for language learning. In Russian 421, students listen to two hours of authentic Russian audio material over the course of each week and submit a written log of their work. The objective of this assignment is to help improve learners' aural word recognition, expand their vocabulary, accustom them to rapid speech and to the sound changes that occur in connected speech, increase familiarity with common language features of spoken Russian, and increase overall proficiency and linguistic confidence.

Before listening, students review a list of pre-listening, listening, and post-listening strategies, based on which they decide how to best approach the listening task at hand, based on their needs and goals. The students are also encouraged to try various strategies in order to see what works best for them. Students find audio materials that suit their interests and goals and listen to at least two hours of authentic Russian speech. Students may listen to all new material for the entire two hours or replay a shorter segment up to six times, as long as the total amount adds up to 120 minutes. During or following the listening, the students record details about each segment (such as title, length in minutes, and source). They also submit a ten-sentence summary (in Russian) of each segment, as well as a list of twenty new words and phrases learned, and a reflection in which they are asked what was easy and difficult about the segment and what strategies they will use the following week to make the assignment more useful. Students are instructed to select material that will be comprehensible but challenging. They may look for material that is personally meaningful and interesting to them and that relates to their college major or professional interests; likewise, they can seek out material that is less familiar and, therefore, may present a challenge and fill a knowledge gap. Finally, students are encouraged to look for materials that are more formal (e.g., from professional news outlets) rather than informal (e.g., from personal blogs), to select reports on current events, and to review ACTFL Advanced- and Superior-level descriptors as well as their language proficiency contracts in order to keep on track.

Intensive Reading

Whereas Russian 421 focuses on extensive listening, Russian 422 employs intensive reading, though students are encouraged to continue extensive listening. Carson (1997, pp. 49-50) notes that extensive reading generally involves rapid reading of large quantities of material for general understanding, focusing on the meaning of the text rather than on the language. Intensive reading, on the other hand, involves working with short texts in order to understand every part of the reading in detail, improve reading skills, and develop vocabulary and grammar knowledge.

Learners at the Advanced level are very skilled at reading for general meaning but frequently are content to get the "gist" of more complicated passages. To promote closer reading in Russian 422, after reading an approximately 5000-word text by way of introduction to a new topic, students are then assigned each night to read two paragraphs of the text with the goal of complete comprehension. In-class assessments include translating complex sentences from Russian into English as accurately as possible, forcing them to go beyond comprehending the main ideas of texts. As they participate in translation, students also learn important words, structures, and turns of phrases that then can be recycled in their own written and spoken Russian.

Activities to Support Development of Linguistic Sophistication

To progress beyond the Advanced level of proficiency, language learners must develop grammatical accuracy and linguistic sophistication. Throughout the fourth-year curriculum, learners engage in a variety of activities designed to support the development of more complex and precise language.

Renderings. According to Shekhtman (2002), learners have a tendency to translate mentally from the L1 to the L2, a process that often results in inaccurate expression in the target language. In order to combat this tendency, Shekhtman advocates a strategy that he calls "simplification," i.e., expressing complex thoughts and ideas simply, using language that the learner already controls. To this end, students in the global debate course are asked to "render" texts from English into Russian. They are specifically forbidden from translating word for word, but, instead, are encouraged to use known structures and lexicon. To gauge progress, students render each text twice—once at the beginning of a unit, and once again towards the end of the unit after they have learned more precise vocabulary collocations and structures.

Written skeleton texts. Although simplification is a useful strategy for language learners to avoid calquing from the L1 to the L2, in order to progress from Advanced towards Superior, learners also must expand their structural and lexical repertoires through another technique that Shekhtman (Ibid.) terms complication. Students are provided with several "skeleton texts" that contain simple sentences and generic vocabulary and are told to flesh out the paragraph by combining sentences and using more precise lexicon. Upon submission of the skeleton text, learners then compare their work with that of a native speaker, thus enabling them to notice the gaps between their language production and that of native speakers.

Students then rewrite their skeleton texts, using the native speaker's text as a model. Instructors use a set of error correction codes to provide feedback on the students' final drafts of renderings and skeleton texts. Rather than correcting each error, instructors code the mistakes as "agreement" mistakes, "aspect" mistakes, etc. Students then work to fix their mistakes. If particular patterns of errors are noticed, instructors suggest supplemental materials and exercises to help learners fix fossilized patterns.

Oral skeleton texts. Oral skeleton texts are similar to written skeleton texts in that they consist of a series of facts that students must connect and communicate, albeit orally. Students record themselves presenting these facts and then compare their recordings against those made by native speakers. Having compared the two recordings, students rerecord the texts while trying to imitate the style of the native speaker.

Extemporaneous monologues. With the advent of new technologies, students can record themselves more easily than ever. In the past few years of the debate course, students have recorded themselves speaking for 3-5 minutes in response to questions related to the debate topic. The questions initially emphasize a personalized and descriptive narrative but become increasingly abstract as learners familiarize themselves with the topic. For instance, when discussing the environment, learners at first are asked whether they consider themselves environmentally conscious. At a later date, they might be asked to describe a particular environmental catastrophe in some detail with an exploration of the underlying causes and consequences. Finally, they begin rehearsing for upcoming debates by arguing for or against a particular motion.

The instructor and a native-speaker Teaching Assistant trained in the ACTFL guidelines listen to every monologue and provide detailed feedback on individual structural errors, as well as suggest more precise vocabulary or more native-like structures for expressing particular ideas. Notes of recurring mistakes are compiled for subsequent targeted instruction and practice. Students are asked to re-record a specified number of monologues in order to fix mistakes, practice new vocabulary and grammatical structures, and embellish their language.

Grammar videos. Leaver and Shekhtman (2002) note that one of the tasks of the language instructor when working with students at the ILR 2/3 threshold is to help learners expand the grammatical models under their command. Learners at this level can use some structures automatically and correctly, other structures automatically but not correctly, and still some structures without automaticity—either because they have not been exposed to or know them only passively. As aforementioned, instructors give attention to learners' errors in written and oral exercises. At the conclusion of each debate unit, learners, in consultation with the instructor, identify particular structures that warrant further study and create an instructional video (usually in the form of a narrated slide show) in which they explain the structure and its usages. The videos are shared with classmates, who can post questions and rate the effectiveness of the video. The videos that the instructor deems most accurate and helpful are added to the course Learning Management System for use by other students, along with suggested resources and exercises for learning a given structure.

Research Projects, Presentations, and Debates.

As part of Russian 421, each student is assigned to participate in three presentations, based on individual, pair, and group research.

Individual presentations. The individual presentations require students to select two or three current events reports from online media outlets (newspapers, television, radio, or podcasts) on such topics as Environment, Science, Healthcare, Sports, Culture, and Information Technology. Media sources are evaluated for reliability based on guidelines discussed in class. Students then prepare an outline and a script for a ten-minute oral presentation, as well as slides containing key terms, key points of their arguments, and a brief overview of sources. To promote creativity, the students are also asked to create a slogan reflecting the purpose of their presentation. The slogan is included in the slides and presented to the audience at the end of the presentation.

Two students present in one day. The class is divided into two groups, and each of the two students addresses one group at a time, with two presentations taking place simultaneously. After a short break, they switch groups and present once again. This format is designed to address the problem of insufficient practice outside of class. It also allows each student to practice in front of a live audience and to compare the two experiences.

Following the presentation, the students write a short reflection essay, in which they answer such questions as: What did I do well? What did I learn from this experience? What did not go as I expected? What is my goal for next time? How can I achieve my goal? After this, the students record themselves delivering the same presentation once more, incorporating peer feedback from class and their own reflections. They upload this presentation to the Learning Management System as a final evidence of a completed project.

During each presentation, students in the audience write down answers to such questions as: (1) What is the topic? (2) What is the thesis? (3) How has my understanding of the topic improved? Or how has my opinion changed as a result of the presentation? (4) What question would I pose to the presenter? A brief discussion follows each presentation, during which members of the audience pose their question to the presenter, and each presenter clarifies or elaborates on their presentation.

Pair presentations. With a partner, students conduct research on a topic, related to one of the themes: Education, Finance, Law, Diplomacy, Military Affairs, or Religion. The preparation stage is similar to that of individual presentations, with the main difference being the need to collaborate with another learner while preparing all the necessary materials: an outline, sources, slides, etc. The students can choose one of three formats for their presentations. The first approach is for each of the two presenters to deliver the same material. Because they only have an outline and not a script, each of them will present in a different manner. The second approach involves splitting the material in two, with each student presenting one half. The challenge of this approach is to create a logical connection between the two halves regardless of the order in which they are presented to two parts of the audience. The third approach involves each partner choosing a side, with one arguing for and the other against the same issue. In this case, the students use the same set of slides, but each must alter the outline to reflect the side that it is defending. Typically, more proficient students choose this approach.

The rest of the format reflects the first presentation, with a few additions. The students are asked to create not only a slogan, but also a meme (the difference between the two is discussed beforehand), and they are also asked to send a survey to their audience a few days after the presentation. The purpose of this survey is to give the students an opportunity to think through the questions that they would like to pose in connection to their research project. During the presentation, students again record themselves and write brief reflections after this experience. Since this time the students do not have a prepared script, they choose a one-minute segment of their audio recording, transcribe and analyze it, and then rewrite it in order to make the language more coherent and sophisticated.

During the partner presentations, the audience has a similar task as before; however, oral questioning is shortened to leave more time for small group discussions during which students perform different tasks from day to day. Over the course of this block of presentations, students are gradually introduced to such notions as confabulation, heuristics of availability, Occam's razor, and others. Students in the audience use these concepts to evaluate the presentations they heard. In particular, they discuss effectiveness of introductions, compare their notes on the arguments and the evidence that were presented, formulate counterarguments, or suggest alternative ways to begin or finish a presentation effectively.

An informal student survey has shown that students see the benefit of presenting the same material twice; practicing beforehand on their own or in front of one person proved insufficient in preparation for speaking in front of a live audience. The presenters saw how differently an audience can react to the same material, and they had to adjust their speaking style accordingly. On the other hand, the audience benefited from hearing the material twice and from seeing how individual approaches differ even when the subject is the same.

Group presentations. The third block of presentations is prepared and delivered in groups of 3-4 students, carefully selected by the instructor in order to achieve a mix of proficiency levels. Students identify an area of knowledge that none of them has presented on and that is not related to their majors or minors. Having been introduced to the concepts of divergent and convergent thinking, students first brainstorm to identify a wide variety of topics and possible research questions for their project, but then narrow their focus to formulate a specific topic that each member of the group can agree on.

As part of their preparation, each group conducts an audience survey. The purpose of the survey is to give the presenters the information that is necessary for tailoring the presentation to the needs and interests of the audience. In order to be persuasive, the students need to not only know their subject, but also who they are speaking to. Students have an opportunity to think critically about the sort of information that they need and what questions they will need to pose to obtain it. Students can ask questions designed to reveal the audience's attitudes, biases, prior knowledge, or special interests in the topic. The groups also can use these surveys as a way to increase the audience's curiosity in each of their research projects.

A large part of the preparation is done in class, over the course of six meetings (or three weeks). The students formulate their thesis statements and begin outlining their arguments and organizing evidence. Once they have initial drafts, students analyze how their outline aligns with the following structure: (1) an introduction that catches the audience's attention, (2) a clear thesis statement, (3) a brief list of main arguments, (4) evidence, and (5) a strong conclusion. Students also consider transitions between arguments and between students' individual parts, attention-getting devices (memes, slogans, video/audio clips, etc.), and timing (20-25 minutes for the whole group). Towards the end of the preparation process, each group gives a brief, three-minute preview of their upcoming presentation to the whole class, providing an opportunity for formative assessment of student progress.

During an actual presentation, students in the audience not only listen for a thesis, arguments, and evidence, but write down their possible counterarguments. Each presentation is followed by fifteen or twenty minutes of questioning, after which students in small groups discuss the substance of the presentation, the quality of arguments, and the effectiveness of performance methods. This practice serves not only as a logical conclusion to the work that the students have done in the Russian 421 course, but also functions as a stepping stone towards the debate format that awaits them in Russian 422.

Debates

Whereas in Russian 421 students focus on presentational speech, in Russian 422 they work towards participating in debates that require a greater ability to think on their feet in order to respond to each other's arguments. In preparation for the debates, students select a "motion" relating to the current topic. Recent motions have included, for example, "The reunification of Crimea with the Russian Federation represents a violation of Ukraine's national sovereignty" and "The United States should build a wall on its southern border to prevent illegal immigration."

Early in the semester, students are introduced to the idea of debate "stases," or types of questions at issue in a debate. For instance, a debate may hinge on questions of definition (e.g., "What constitutes national sovereignty?") or questions of value (e.g., "Is it fair to deny people access to a better life in a richer country?"), among other types of questions. Students brainstorm different types of questions for each topic. They also listen to recorded formal debates and identify the types of questions used by the speakers.

As students begin to prepare for the debates, they are put into teams of 3 or 4 and assigned to argue for or against a particular motion. First, students identify the main questions at issue in the debate and formulate their answers as well as consider potential counterarguments. For example, when students debated the reunification of Crimea with Russia, much of the debate hinged on definitions of sovereignty and nation. In groups, students decide which arguments they are going to make and in what order. They write out their main arguments, list potential counterarguments, and consider how to respond to the counterarguments, while also using the rhetorical devices learned in Russian 421 and Russian 422.

Recorded parliamentary debates on YouTube serve as useful models. Students watch these debates several times, first, to identify the debate stases, then to identify the main arguments, and also to identify particular rhetorical devices, e.g., how are counterarguments introduced. At various points throughout the semester, students are asked to listen to one speaker's argument and then to respond immediately.

Professional Internships in the Context of Studying Russian

An important ancillary to the fourth-year Russian curriculum at BYU is the internship program. Although the internship is not a requirement for the major, the goals and methods associated therewith align well with those of the fourth-year curriculum.

The Russian internship program for BYU students has been running for thirteen years. It began with a collaboration between BYU and the Moscow Higher School of Social and Economic Sciences (MHSSES) and, in 2016, was expanded to include Riga, Latvia and, specifically, the Baltic Center for Educational and Academic Development. The program is unique in that it provides students with a high-degree of proficiency in Russian with the opportunity to participate in professional internships in Russian-speaking private- and public-sector companies and organizations. In addition, students receive advanced level language instruction in a format similar to Russian 422.

In recent years, the range of professional internships available to BYU students has expanded considerably and now encompasses such fields as jurisprudence, human rights, history, genealogy, philology, pedagogy, medicine, business, finance, science, computer technology, athletics, and graphic design. The human rights and humanitarian society "Memorial," International Genealogical Center, Tsaritsyno Museum-Reserve, Skolkovo Institute of Science and Technology (Skoltech), Slavic Center for Law and Justice, Public Auction Organization (PAO) Group Cherkizovo (the largest producer and processor of poultry and pork in Russia), Center for the Promotion of Reform of Criminal Justice "Prison and Will," European Medical Center, Humanitarian Fund "Children of Maria," and others all have invited BYU students to intern with them.

In addition to pursuing full-time internships, students attend advanced foreign language courses twice a week (six hours total) at the Moscow Higher School of Social and Economic Sciences and the Baltic Center for Educational and Academic Development. The curriculum for the language course is based on the textbook Mastering Russian Through Global Debate (Brown, Balykhina, Talalakina, Bown, & Kurilenko, 2014). To avoid any overlap with the on-campus 422 course, which uses the same textbook, the internship debate course covers the last three chapters of the textbook, while the on-campus course focuses on the first three.

Prior to going abroad, students complete an ACTFL computer-adapted Oral Proficiency Interview (OPIc) and shortly before returning to the states, they complete a post-OPIc in order to ascertain the degree to which their language skills improved while participating on the program. Since some students on the program have not completed the 421 or 422 course prior to departure, the program director instructs them in the ACTFL proficiency guidelines, particularly as they relate to professional-level proficiency and beyond. Having received such instruction and their pre-OPIc ratings, students are able both to pinpoint their strengths and weaknesses and to target specific areas on which to focus. Accordingly, in addition to receiving formal language instruction, students carry out an array of professional roles, including such roles as athletic trainer, English-language teacher, event organizer, medical assistant, business consultant, manager, translator, statistical analyst, and so forth. By working in teams with Russian colleagues, they carry out activities that require a variety of communicative skills on the professional level.

While in country, students also complete a Canvas course that builds on strengths from the American Council on the Teaching of Foreign Languages Integrated Performance Assessment and engages them in real-world tasks designed to improve language proficiency, cultural awareness, and professional development within a single theme or content area. The course focuses on helping students recognize and develop four key global professional competencies: (1) foreign language proficiency (domain specific professional language), (2) intercultural awareness/cross-cultural competence, (3) intercultural collaboration and teamwork, and (4) intercultural professional communication.

Each competency offers specific ways for students to take ownership of their internship and to increase their self-awareness as a burgeoning professional. Students are instructed to approach each assignment as a chance to "try on" each competency with the understanding that some will fit better than others. The goal is for students to identify specific behaviors that will help them make the most of their internship as a high-stakes experience. In addition, they are to demonstrate their understanding of field-specific professional Russian, key global competencies, and the ability to translate the value of such competencies in professional contexts through vocabulary development exercises, an interview with a subject matter expert, and a video presentation.

Mastering a specialized language involves building a substantial lexical base. While program instructors work closely with participants in the classroom and conduct individual consultations as needed, the majority of language instruction falls on the shoulders of the students themselves and their internship supervisors. Experience suggests that a professional environment lends itself to more rapid and successful acquisition of specialized terminology. Noticeable progress also has been observed in participants' analytical reading skills. Of course, practicing this type of reading also can be done in the classroom, but a real-world setting makes this task more relevant and, thus, more effective. Past experience also confirms that internships have a positive influence on student participation during class instruction. Professional engagement together with context-based instruction (e.g., teaching materials, methods, and tools that approximate the professional dealings of an intern) add a personal element to the process of studying a language and afford opportunities for accomplishing career-related goals.

Acquiring circumstance-appropriate speech (e.g., understanding how to converse with colleagues and clients, patients in the hospital, students and their parents, etc.) also serves as an important goal for student interns. In addition to acquiring specialized terminology, students who join a Russian-speaking team acquire professional jargon. For example, past interns who worked in the field of computer technology initially tried to come up with Russian equivalents for English verbs, but eventually followed their Russian colleagues' example and adopted loanwords from English, e.g., *attachit'* (from "attach"), *apgreidit'* (from "upgrade"), and *apruvit'* (from "approve"). Such easily acquired IT jargon not only helps interns feel comfortable on a Russian-speaking team, but also illustrates the productivity of Russian word formation.

Differences in US and Russian work environments often necessitate comprehensive study of specific topics for interns. By way of example, past medical interns needed to acquaint themselves with the healthcare system in the Russian Federation, specifics of treating patients in medical and healthcare facilities, and medical specializations and duties. Familiarizing themselves with the medical field requires independent research and analysis on their part and substantive discussions with Russian colleagues, which serve to develop their professional, linguistic, and cultural knowledge. Topics selected by students include such matters as duties of a physician's assistant in Russia and the US and the educational level and functional requirements of a paramedic and general practitioner in both countries.

Limitations and Directions for Future Research

Although the curriculum for students interning abroad includes a journaling exercise intended to develop intercultural competence, connecting this exercise with the actual debate curriculum remains to be done, as does an examination of possible cultural difference and intercultural communicative competence through the lens of debate. Currently the fourth-year curriculum prioritizes linguistic competence but plans also are underway to address intercultural competence by focusing on differences in debate styles between Western and Russian traditions.

Conclusion

This paper describes the implementation of the fourth-year curriculum at Brigham Young University. A curriculum in which learning tasks are aligned with desired proficiency outcomes and which provides scaffolding to complete those tasks can have a significant impact on learners' linguistic outcomes. Moreover, the program is designed to enhance research skills, information literacy, sociocultural competence, and metacognitive skills—all of which contribute to life-long learning beyond the university. The addition of professional internships, combined with in-country study of the L2 and targeted self-instruction in domain-specific vocabulary not only facilitates language learning, but also leads to development of professional skills important to participate in an increasingly globalized world.

References

Aclan, E. M., & Aziz, N. H. A. (2015). Exploring parliamentary debate as a pedagogical tool to develop English communication skills in EFL/ESL classrooms. *International Journal of Applied Linguistics and English Literature* 4(2): 1-16.

American Council on the Teaching of Foreign Languages. (2012). *ACTFL Proficiency Guidelines – Speaking*. Downloaded from https://www.actfl.org/resources/actfl-proficiency-guidelines-2012/english/speaking.

American Council on the Teaching of Foreign Languages. *Assigning CEFR Ratings to ACTFL Assessments.* Downloaded from https://www.actfl.org/sites/default/files/reports/Assigning_CEFR_Ratings_To_ACTFL_Assessments.pdf

Brecht, R. D., Davidson, E., & Ginsberg, R. B. (1993). *Predictors of foreign language gain during study abroad*. Washington, D.C.: Occasional Papers of the National Foreign Language Center.

Brown, N. A. (2009). Argumentation and debate in foreign language instruction: A case for the traditional classroom facilitating advanced level language uptake. *Modern Language Journal, 93*(4), 534-549.

Brown, N. A., Solovieva, R. V., & Eggett, D. L. (2011). Qualitative and quantitative measures of second language writing: Potential outcomes of informal target language learning abroad. *Foreign Language Annals* 44(1): 105-121.

Brown, T., Balykhina, T., Talalakina, E., Bown, J., & Kurilenko, V. (2014). *Mastering Russian through global debate*. Washington, D.C.: Georgetown University Press.

Brown, N. A., Talalakina, E. V., Yakusheva, I. V. & Eggett, D. L. (2012). Argumentation and debate in the foreign language classroom: Russian and American university students collaborating through new technologies. *Russian Language Journal 62*: 141-166.

Connor, U. (1987). Argumentative patterns in student essays: Cross-cultural differences. In U. Connor & R. Kaplan (Eds.), *Writing across languages*: Analysis of L2 text (pp. 57–71). Boston, MA: Addison-Wesley.

Conway, W. D. (1976). Debate in the TESL Classroom. *TESOL Quarterly 10*(3): 305-308.

Davidson, D. (2002). When just being there is not enough. *UW–Madison Global Forum Symposium on Language Gain and Study Abroad*. Madison, WI.

Donato, R., & Brooks, F. (2004). Literary discussions and advanced speaking functions: Researching the (dis)connection. *Foreign Language Annals 37*: 183–199.

Duncombe, S., & Heikkinen, M. H. (1988). Role-playing for different viewpoints. *College Teaching 36*(1): 3-5.

Ehrman, M. (2002a). Teachers and students at the threshold of four-level proficiency. *ACTR Letter 28*(3): 1-3.

Ehrman, M. (2002b). The learner at the Superior-Distinguished threshold. In B. L. Leaver & B. S. Shekhtman (Eds.), *Developing professional-level language proficiency* (pp. 245-259). Cambridge, UK: Cambridge University Press.

Elliot, L. B. (1993). Using debates to teach the psychology of women. *Teaching of Psychology 20*(1): 35-38.

Engeström, Y. (2005). Non scolae sed vitae discimus: Toward overcoming the encapsulation of school learning. In H. Daniels (Ed.), *An introduction to Vygotsky* (2nd ed., pp. 157-176). London: Routledge.

Fauzan, U. (2016). Enhancing speaking ability of EFL students through debate and peer assessment. *EFL Journal 1*(1): 49-57.

Freels, S., Kisselev, O., & Alsufieva, A. (2017). Adding breadth to the undergraduate curriculum: Flagship approaches to interdisciplinary language learning. In D. Murphy & K. Evans-Romaine (Eds.), *Exploring the US language flagship program: Professional competence in a second language by graduation* (pp. 51-69). Bristol, UK: Multilingual Matters.

Frodesen, J., & Holten, C. (2003). Grammar and the ESL writing class. In B. Kroll (Ed.), *Exploring the dynamics of second language writing* (pp. 141-161). Cambridge, UK: Cambridge University Press.

Gregory, M., & Holloway, M. (2005). The debate as a pedagogic tool in social policy for social work students. *Social Work Education 24*(6): 617-637.

Hartwell, P. (1985). Grammar, grammars, and the teaching of grammar. *College English 47*: 105-127.

Hedegaard, M. (2005). The Zone of proximal development as basis for instruction. In H. Daniels (Ed.), *An introduction to Vygotsky* (2nd ed., pp. 227-251). London: Routledge.

Higgs, T. V., & Clifford, R. T. (1982). The push toward communication. *Curriculum competence and the foreign language teacher. ACTFL Foreign Language Education Series 13*: 57-59.

Iman, J. N. (2017). Debate instruction in EFL classroom: Impacts on the critical thinking and speaking skill. *International Journal of Instruction 10*(4): 87-108.

Inch, E. S., & Warnick, B. (2005). *Critical thinking and communication: The use of reason in argument* (5th ed.). Allyn and Bacon.

Jourdenais, R. M., & Shaw, P.A. (2005). Dimensions of content-based instruction in second language education. In R. M. Jourdenais & P. A. Shaw (Eds.), *Content, tasks, and projects in the language classroom: 2004 conference proceedings* (pp. 1-12). Monterey, CA: Monterey Institute of International Studies.

Leaver, B. L., & Shekhtman, B. (2002). Principles and practices in teaching Superior-level language skills: not just more of the same. In B. L. Leaver & B. Shekhtman (Eds.), *Developing professional-level language proficiency* (pp. 3-33). Cambridge, UK: Cambridge University Press.

Long, M. H. (2007). *Problems in SLA*. Hillsdale, NJ: Lawrence Erlbaum Associates, Publishers.

Massie, J. (2005). Consideration of context in the CBI course development process. In R. M. Jourdenais & S. E. Springer (Eds.), *Content, tasks and projects in the language classroom: 2004 conference proceedings* (pp. 79–91). Monterey, CA: Monterey Institute of International Studies.

MLA Ad Hoc Committee on Foreign Languages. (2007). *Foreign language and higher education: New structures for a changed world.* New York: The Modern Language Association of America.

Morley, J. (2005). Issues in teaching phonetics/pronunciation at advanced levels of instruction in English as a Foreign Language. *Journal for Distinguished Language Studies 3*: 9-14.

Musselman, E. G. (2004). Using structured debate to achieve autonomous student discussion. *The History Teacher 37*(3): 335-349.

Osborne, A. (2005). Debate and student development in the history classroom. *New directions for teaching and learning 2005*(103): 39-50.

Redding, W. C. (1954). Composition of the debate speech. In D. Potter (Ed.), *Argumentation and debate: Principles and practices* (pp. 193–213). Hinsdale, IL: The Dryden Press.

Roy, A., & Macchiette, B. (2005). Debating the issues: A tool for augmenting critical thinking skills of marketing students. *Journal of Marketing Education 27*(3): 264-276.

Shaw, P. A. (1997). With one stone: Models of instruction and their curricular implications in an advanced content-based foreign language program. In S. B. Stryker & B. L. Leaver (Eds.), *Content-based instruction in foreign language education: Models and methods* (pp. 261-282). Washington, DC: Georgetown University Press.

Shekhtman, B. (2005). Do Superior-level students need language instruction? An essay in answer to the myth of natural acquisition and self-study being sufficient at high levels of foreign language acquisition. *ACTR Letter 3*: 71-78.

Shekhtman, B., Lord, N., & Kuznetsova, E. (2003). Complication exercises for raising the oral proficiency level of highly advanced language students. *Journal for Distinguished Language Studies 1*(1): 31-50.

Shekhtman, B., & Leaver, B. L. with Lord, N., Kuznetsova, E., & Ovtcharenko, E. (2002). Developing professional-level oral proficiency: The Shekhtman method of communicative teaching. In B. L. Leaver & B. Shekhtman (Eds.), *Developing professional-level language proficiency* (pp. 119-140). Cambridge, UK: Cambridge University Press.

Stokes, P.M. (1976). Debating in the ESL classroom. *ELT Journal 31*(1): 15-17.

Stryker, S. B, & Leaver, B. L. (1997). Content-based instruction: From theory to practice. In S. B. Stryker, & B. L. Leaver (Eds.), *Content-based instruction in foreign language education: Models and methods* (pp. 3-28). Washington, DC: Georgetown University Press.

Swain, M. (1993). The Output Hypothesis: Just speaking and writing aren't enough. *The Canadian Modern Language Review/La Revue canadienne des langues vivantes* 50: 158–164.

Tavakoli, R., Aliasin, S. H., & Mobini, F. (2017). The effect of structured academic controversy on English proficiency level within communicative language teaching context. *Journal of Language Teaching and Research 8*(2): 349-354.

Tumposky, N. R. (2004). The debate debate. *The Clearing House: A Journal of Educational Strategies, Issues and Ideas 78*(2): 52-56.

van Lier, L. (2005). The bellman's map: Avoiding the "perfect and absolute blank" in language learning. In R. M. Jourdenais, & P. A. Shaw (Eds.), *Content, tasks and projects in the language classroom: 2004 conference proceedings* (pp. 13-21). Monterey, CA: Monterey Institute of International Studies.

Vo, H. X., & Morris, R. L. (2006). Debate as a tool in teaching economics: Rationale, technique, and some evidence. *Journal of Education for Business, 81*(6), 315-320.

Whitehead, A. N. (1929). *The aims of education*. London: Macmillan.

Wolfe-Quintero, K., Inagaki, S., & Kim, H. (1998). *Second language development in writing: Measures of fluency, accuracy, and complexity*. O'ahu, HI: University of Hawai'i Press.

Zare, P., & Othman, M. (2015). Students' perceptions toward using classroom debate to develop critical thinking and oral communication ability. *Asian Social Science 11*(9): 158.

21st Century Skills Map--World Languages. (2011). *Partnership for 21st century skills*. Downloaded from https://www.actfl.org/sites/default/files/resources/21st%20Century%20Skills%20Map-World%20Languages.pdf.\

The Challenge of the Inverted Pyramid in Attaining Distinguished-Level Proficiency

Andrew R. Corin

Defense Language Institute Foreign Language Center (USA)

Abstract

Drawing on imagery from a 1985 contribution by Pardee Lowe, Jr., this article frames the quest for Distinguished-level L2 proficiency as the ascent from the foot of a mountain to the summit (near-native or Distinguished-level proficiency). Success in this quest depends crucially on two conditions: (1) reaching the base camp (around Superior-level proficiency) with sufficient time, and (2) with the equipment needed for the final ascent. For this to have any likelihood of occurring more broadly than at present, it is necessary to somehow defeat the phenomenon known as the inverted pyramid. This in turn requires us to probe the reality that underlies this metaphorical construct. Once we understand its nature, shape and causes, the way forward becomes clearer, and there are in fact specific instructional and curricular design approaches that can help us mitigate, if not entirely eliminate it. One of these, a modular open architecture approach to curricular design, is described in Section 2, and a hypothesis is formulated as to one mechanism through which it appears to mitigate the inverted pyramid phenomenon. Section 3 surveys the origin and history of the inverted pyramid construct before turning to an examination of its substance, shape, and slope. The final two subsections summarize the causes of the inverted pyramid phenomenon and realistic approaches to defeating it, which include the curricular approach described in Section 2.

Keywords: Distinguished-level language proficiency; Interagency Language Roundtable Level 4 language proficiency; inverted pyramid of proficiency growth; modular curriculum; open architecture curricular design

1. Introduction

This article has its genesis in a recent book chapter (Corin, 2021) in which I describe one model of modular open architecture curricular design (OACD) developed and implemented across multiple languages at the U.S. Defense Language Institute Foreign Language Center (DLIFLC) between 2012-2014. The purpose underpinning its design was to enable rapid design and deployment of short, high impact courses that would allow for substantive ongoing modification in real time and enable proficiency growth across a broad range of incoming proficiency profiles in uncharacteristically short time frames. I hypothesized that one of the reasons why this approach yielded learning outcomes superior to those expected from "traditional" (i.e., organized according to linear scope and sequence) textbook courses in similar circumstances was that it appeared to be countering the inverted pyramid phenomenon in a very specific way.

Strategies to enable broader and more rapid attainment of Distinguished-level proficiency depend upon a clear understanding of the nature of this metaphorical construct. The present essay therefore provides grounding for the hypothesis posited in Corin (2021) by tying it to a range of questions concerning the history, validation, structure, and universality of the inverted pyramid construct.

The quest for Distinguished-level second language (L2) proficiency leads us in fact toward a confluence of metaphors. To begin, we may view this quest through the lens of Lowe's (1985b) metaphor of an ascent toward the summit (near-native proficiency) of a mountain. Lowe introduced this metaphor primarily to illustrate the differing perspectives of researchers focusing on the base of the mountain, the base camp further up (around ILR 3) and the summit of near-native L2 proficiency. This same metaphor serves admirably, though, to make two of the four primary takeaway points of this paper in regard to the actual L2 learning process: that success in achieving the summit depends critically on reaching the base camp quickly enough to enable an ascent, and on arriving there with the equipment for the final ascent firmly in place. Success in the quest depends furthermore on defeating two metaphorical pyramids, one inverted and the other not. The "inverted pyramid," as a metaphor for the difficulty of attaining ever higher-level, and especially Distinguished-level, proficiency is well known. Imagining an ascent up a cliff face with a flaring overhang as one approaches the summit (as suggested by early depictions of the inverted pyramid) can help drive home the difficulty of the endeavor. On this occasion I will be introducing the further metaphor of a non-inverted pyramid of time-on-task with ever higher levels of tasks and texts as an impediment to reaching the base camp in a timely manner. Along the route to the summit we will encounter both hares and tortoises attempting the ascent, resting at different points along the way and filling buckets as they go.

In Section 2, I will review the manner in which modular OACD appeared to be countering both the inverted pyramid and non-inverted pyramid through a strategy that I term "vertical spiraling." In Section 3, I will examine a number of key questions related to the history, validation and shape of the inverted pyramid, as well as the sources of the phenomenon, in order to illuminate how they affect our striving to enable learners to achieve Distinguished (ILR 4 and higher) L2 proficiency. A third takeaway will be that despite its ubiquity in graphic representations of language proficiency, its enduring usefulness, and broad acceptance by many L2 professionals as a fact of life of L2 learning, the inverted pyramid construct and its ramifications have been the object of relatively little research. Finally, in Subsection 3.5 I will identify realistic approaches—a majority already recognized as current or emerging best practices—toward mitigating the inverted pyramid as a phenomenon of L2 learning that puts Distinguished-level proficiency beyond the reach of many learners. One curricular approach is modular vertically spiraled OACD as illustrated in Section 2. A fourth takeaway will thus be that we are by no means powerless to mitigate, if not in fact to overcome, the limitation described by the inverted pyramid.

2. OACD and the Inverted Pyramid

One of the ways in which modular OACD (Campbell et al., 2017; Campbell, 2021; Corin, 1997, 2020a, 2020b, 2021; Dababneh, 2018; Derderian, (2017); Krasner, 2018) promotes rapid proficiency growth is suggested by Figure 1 (which reproduces Corin, 2021, Figure 6.3). Both pyramids in this figure are of course substantial simplifications. "Linear scope and sequence" refers to the sequenced introduction of specific linguistic and paralinguistic (pragmatic, discourse, sociocultural, rhetorical) elements as well as task and text types. It is more-or-less what a traditional textbook does, especially at lower levels of study.

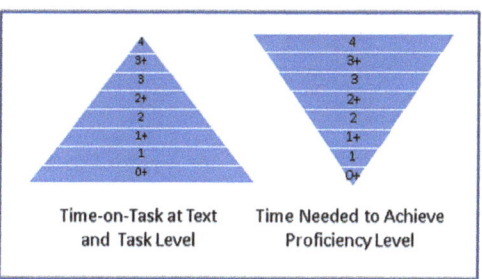

Fig. 1. The Inverted and Noninverted Pyramids under Linear Scope and Sequence Reproduced from Corin in Leaver et al., *Transformative Language Learning and Teaching*, Cambridge University Press, copyright 2021, p. 57.

One inherent limitation of this approach (leaving aside the limits that it places on flexibility) is that it tends to restrict, progressively, the time-on-task that learners have with progressively higher-level text and task types, as well as with specific linguistic and paralinguistic elements associated primarily with them. The higher the level of text or task, the less time-on-task learners will have with it. In such an environment, if one attempts to introduce too high-level a text or task, it typically generates complaints of the form "but we haven't had that word (tense, case, etc.) yet" or "but we haven't learned how to do that yet." Linear scope and sequence would naturally tend to reinforce, if not in part to create, an inverted pyramid of proficiency growth.

Modular OACD eliminates linear sequencing of text/task types and specific linguistic/paralinguistic elements (but not all elements of sequencing; see Dababneh, 2018; Corin, 2020b, 2021), and in so doing mitigates the problematic non-inverted pyramid. What this means is that aside from other more obvious benefits of OACD (easier/more rapid development, deployment, and modification to meet learner need) it should also, in principle, promote accelerated attainment of proficiency, at least in this particular respect, and especially at the upper ranges.

So, how does this work? Figure 2 (which reproduces Corin, 2021, Figure 6.2) provides a diagram (highly simplified, to be sure) of how the non-inverted pyramid works in practice. The progression refers not just to task types,[50] but also to the text types associated with them, as well as to the sequenced introduction of linguistic and paralinguistic elements associated with ever higher-level text and task types.

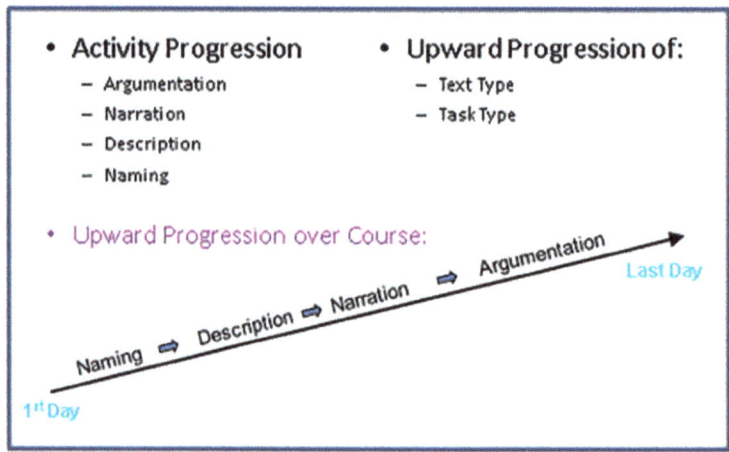

Fig. 2. Progression under Linear Scope and Sequence
Reproduced from Corin in Leaver et al., *Transformative Language Learning and Teaching*, Cambridge University Press, copyright 2021, p. 56.

---

50   In Figures 2 and 3, "description" refers not to the minimally cohesive descriptive discourse described by the ILR and ACTFL proficiency level descriptions as a characteristic of Advanced (ILR 2), but rather to isolated descriptive statements within the reach of Intermediate (ILR 1) speakers.

Now, let's say that instead of programming this progression between the first and last day of a course, we shorten it to progressing from lowest to highest level between the first and last day of each month, after which the same progression is repeated. Or, instead of abbreviating the progression to monthly cycles, we reduce it to weekly, daily, or even hourly cycles. The ever-shorter time frame of each progression yields a cyclic movement as portrayed in Figure 3 (which reproduces Corin, 2021, Figure 6.1). It still yields a progression over the length of the course, but it is no longer one of text and task types; it has now been transformed into a progression of performance at all text/task levels.

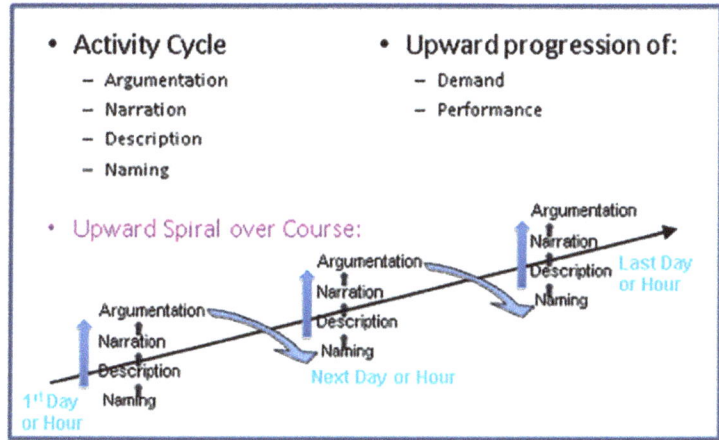

Fig. 3. Progression in a Vertical Spiraling Context
Reproduced from Corin in Leaver et al., *Transformative Language Learning and Teaching*, Cambridge University Press, copyright 2021, p. 56.

I refer to this cyclic progression as vertical spiraling. It consists of a cyclic repetition of series of tasks/activities of ever-increasing complexity based on authentic materials relevant to the task. In each iteration learners achieve incrementally greater skill in performing tasks and working with texts at each level, either within or across differing content areas. To be sure, during early iterations learners' performance with higher-level text and task types may be limited, even rudimentary, depending on their incoming proficiency profile. Working with higher-level authentic texts than learners' proficiency level entails a "fit-the-task-to-the-text" rather than a "fit-the-text-to-the-task" approach.

The traditional concept of spiraling in curricular organization is based on a periodic recycling of content areas. During each iteration, learners achieve greater breadth and depth of understanding. In vertical spiraling, instead of cycling through content areas, learners cycle vertically through levels of task and, to some extent, text complexity. The two forms of spiraling are mutually compatible.

Within a vertical spiraling approach, learners' exposure to and time-on-task with higher-level text/task types, together with their associated linguistic and paralinguistic elements, would naturally tend to approach their exposure and time-on-task working with lower-level text/task types. Vertical spiraling would therefore be predicted to counter, to some degree, the inverted pyramid phenomenon.

Vertical spiraling thus programs into the curriculum, by design, a phenomenon that no doubt occurs to some extent during L2 learning within any instructional/curricular approach, only less systematically, so that its effect may be smaller. The approach can be illustrated by Clifford's (2016) bucket analogy (see Figure 4), which we can extend to encompass Distinguished-level proficiency. Vertical spiraling ensures that the higher-level buckets are being filled simultaneously with the lower-level ones and attempts to even out the rate at which they are filled.

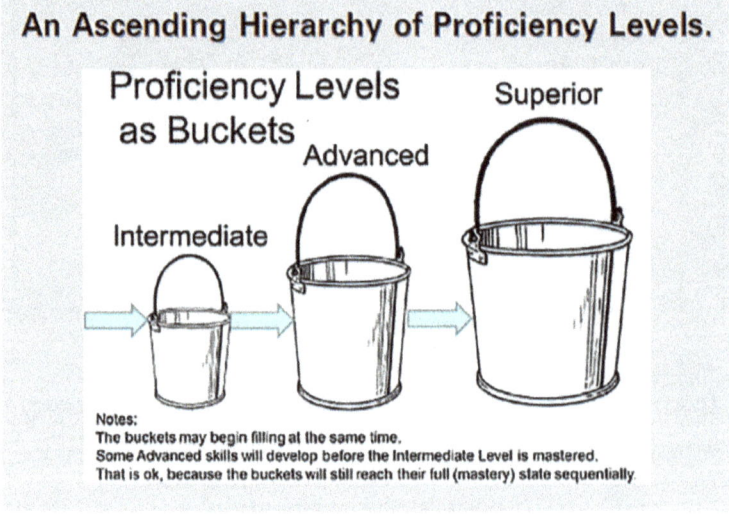

Fig. 4. An Ascending Hierarchy of ProficiencyLevels
Reproduced from Clifford, "A Rationale for Criterion-Referenced Proficiency Testing," *Foreign Language Annals*, published by the American Council on Teaching Foreign Languages, copyright 2016, Wiley & Sons, p. 230.

Vertical spiraling also operationalizes the admonition that instructors should not be so worried about what their students "can't" do (they very likely can, just not as well at first), and that they should not place a glass ceiling over them by limiting the tasks that they allow them to attempt.[51] After all, how much proficiency is really required for learners to begin to express and support opinion? Proficiency in supporting opinion on topics at a societal level is characteristic of ILR Level 3 (Su-

---

51 This is a paraphrase from my notes of comments by Tarone (2017) at a workshop on language teacher education.

perior). Yet all one really needs to express opinion in a rudimentary way is a phrase corresponding to "I believe/think" and the ability to express a simple proposition, which need not be grammatically correct nor even be easily comprehensible to native speakers. To support opinion, one similarly requires no more than "because" and the ability to express, in however rudimentary a form, a simple proposition. Learners can thus begin to express and support opinion no later than ILR 0+ (Novice High). Performance will be rudimentary, but it can be enhanced incrementally over innumerable iterative rehearsals with feedback long before learners reach a sustainable ILR Level 2 (Advanced). As Stevick (1971, p. 65) emphasized in his discussion of curricular adaptation, "... any topic may be treated at any degree of linguistic difficulty, from the simplicity of 'What is this? It is a (papilla, colony, Petri dish, centrifuge, etc.)' to the complexity of 'The never before published volume lying at an angle of approximately 37° to the edge of the table is wholly supported by it.'"

Vertically spiraled OACD has proven efficacious in a number of particularly challenging course design and instructional situations at DLIFLC. Corin (1997, 2021) provides two striking illustrations of the degree of success that can be achieved even in adverse instructional circumstances. Since these have been described on multiple occasions in addition to those cited here, I will present only a brief overview. No textbook was utilized in any of the situations described.

In the first instance—a conversion course to convert Czech proficiency to proficiency in Serbian-Croatian—a modular scenario-based instructional approach was applied in which vertical spiraling stands out in an especially transparent form (Corin, 1997). For all scenario-based modules, the students themselves first generated the situations, objectives within those situations, and the military schemata for carrying them out. Later, they would go on to generate multiple situation cards for each role as well as for the global circumstances (current situation on the ground, rules of engagement, logistical circumstances, and so on).

In the meantime, with instructors assisting in a primarily facilitating role, work-up would begin from brainstorming at the lexical level as to the vocabulary and phraseology likely to be useful, then collocations, situations and interactions likely to occur and approaches to dealing with them, contextual and sociocultural points, up to the point of trying out the scenario from students' desks. After debriefing and troubleshooting, they would try again. Realism was gradually introduced into the setting for subsequent rehearsals by first removing class furniture, and finally moving to the most realistic setting possible with as many props as students could muster. For the car search exercise,[52] this involved performing the scenario in a parking lot with real vehicles, non-functional but realistic-looking weapon props, contraband, native speaker drivers, and so on.

---

52 To the best of my knowledge, this was the first usage of what was to become a "classic" military language training scenario.

As the realism of the setting increased, ever more unexpected complications would arise—linguistic, practical, sociocultural, and psychological—all of which required troubleshooting and solutions, which in turn raised the level of the language utilized for this process. For example, real automobiles have real windows which can be either up and down; drivers have hands which you either can or cannot see. Opening real doors has real consequences, etc. Contextual (e.g., weather) and sociocultural differences that seemed abstract in a classroom revealed critical real-life ramifications.

What this yielded was a cyclic learning process in which students would gradually, in phases, work up to a performance, following which they would undergo a debrief and troubleshooting session, followed by work-up to another performance of the scenario. Not only did this cyclic process of work-up ➔ performance ➔ debrief/troubleshooting yield an incremental enhancement of linguistic performance; it also yielded an upward curve in students' ability to integrate linguistic and non-linguistic performance (initially rudimentary at best), as well as to negotiate the affective demands of simulated ambiguity and adversity, including danger. One significant discovery was that these additional non-linguistic demands degraded linguistic performance, severely at first, making their integration into the training crucial. Use of situation cards for the various roles and circumstances yielded an essentially infinite range of scenario variation, so that they could be performed numerous times, if desired, without becoming tedious.

While such scenario-based modules were not the only approach utilized during this course (others including primarily content-based modules, media analysis, and some grammatical analysis later in the course, all done in target-language only with authentic materials), they clearly played a significant role. Not surprisingly, given the emphasis on performance in a scenario-based environment with vertical spiraling, oral proficiency outcomes in 11th-week testing exceeded reading and listening outcomes, with two ILR Level 3 outcomes and a number of 2+ and 2 outcomes among the forty students.

Campbell et al. (2017) and Corin (2021) describe a more complex application initiated between 2012 and 2014 at DLIFLC for two types of learners: one at approximately ILR Level 1+ and the other at Level 2 and above. In this application, content-based learning (CBL) was integrated with scenario-based learning (SBL) through high-level culminating scenarios in one-week modules. Within each module we sought to integrate all activities through their contribution to the culminating scenario as well as reinforcing one another, and to maximally integrate the activities of all learners at all stages of the module. Preparation for the culminating scenario through numerous task performances throughout the week, each incrementally building the knowledge base and perfecting the skills that would be needed, also created a pattern of vertical spiraling, which was then "force-multiplied" by repeating this pattern over and over through successive modules. The "template" described in Corin (2021) was distilled from analogous OACD approaches, in which vertical spiraling played a substantial role, developed and applied over the decade beginning in 2006 in DLIFLC "intermediate" and "advanced" courses, leading to a situation in which ILR 3+ and ILR 4 outcomes had become routine occurrences, albeit not yet regular and not in every cohort.

Models of OACD that share substantial elements with the approaches described above have no doubt been applied by numerous instructors at many institutions over the years. One notable early example is the Foreign Service Institute (FSI) "Bridges" program (School of Language Studies, 1986), to which many others could be added.

A number of potential concerns might be envisaged within such a curricular design. First, within the "purer" vertically spiraled OACD applied in 1993, learners with a primarily ectenic[53] learning style tended to experience some difficulty adjusting to this approach, which required remediation. Within the later SBL-CBL approach, this tended to occur initially for some learners entering with low (around ILR 1+) proficiency who had no previous experience learning through analogous approaches, but these learners generally adapted successfully. In large part, the approach has had quite a positive motivational impact on learners; for example, most find it empowering that they can derive task-relevant usefulness from texts above their current proficiency level. Nevertheless, learning style variables must be addressed to ensure that this conclusion is generalized to all learners. Attention to this parameter of learning is in fact one of the foundational principles of OACD (see Campbell, 2021; Corin, 2020a, 2020b).

One further potential area of concern with the vertically spiraled OACD approach, so described, could concern whether it promotes fossilization of learned error among some students, especially those with low incoming proficiency levels. Design of the approach was informed by an acute awareness of the "terminal 2" profile laid out by Higgs and Clifford (1982). There is as yet no body of research on which to base empirical conclusions in this regard in relation to this form of curricular design. Experience to date applying the model—in challenging instructional contexts, moreover—has provided no reason to believe that this is an actual problem. It is worth bearing in mind that a tendency toward fossilized patterned error is associated with cognitive and learning style, with some learners typically displaying a tendency to fossilize regardless of instructional approach, while others seem to resist fossilization. The emphasis within the modular OACD approach on maximizing the number of vertically spiraled cycles of "work-up ➔ performance ➔ feedback/troubleshooting" (i.e., performance training cycles) with the goal of promoting incremental enhancement in performance builds ongoing opportunities to remediate into the process. More generally, it should be borne in mind that

---

53   "Ectenic" and "synoptic" cognitive or learning styles are understood in the sense of Ehrman and Leaver (2003).

while absence of linear scope and sequence, vertical spiraling, and absence of a textbook are typical and salient features of OACD, the approach is built around a far broader range of best practices (Campbell, 2021; Corin, 2020b), most of which in one manner or another tend to promote learning style neutrality, strategy building, and forestalling fossilization.

3. The Inverted Pyramid Construct

The explanation provided above for the efficiency of modular vertically spiraled OACD—in the situations described—relies in part on its purported effect on the phenomenon known as the inverted pyramid. Now we will examine a series of questions concerning the experiential and (to the extent possible) theoretical underpinnings of the inverted pyramid construct, and will attempt to show how the answers bear on our efforts to enable more learners to attain Distinguished-level L2 proficiency, especially within their organized courses of study.

3.1. Origin and History of the Inverted Pyramid Concept

Sources of the inverted pyramid concept may be found in a variety of experiences. Carroll's (1967) study, which "showcased" the failure of L2 education in the United States to bring even foreign language majors to useful levels of L2 proficiency in four years of college/university study, might already be seen as suggestive of the working of an inverted pyramid. Similar thoughts no doubt occurred to numerous L2 professionals based upon their observations of the performance of generation after generation of students. Systematic attempts to scale the difficulty of attaining particular levels of L2 proficiency became inevitable during the 1970s as an entailment of the nascent L2 proficiency movement, with its push toward quantification of proficiency outcomes beyond the United States Government (USG) context.

Possibly the first essay in this endeavor was Vincent (1978), in which the author attempted "to bring…psychophysical tools to bear on the matter of scaling the difficulty of learning a foreign language" (Vincent, 1978, p. 232). His investigation arose, surprisingly, out of psychophysical research into the relation of the real vs. perceived strength of sensory stimuli such as "loudness, brightness, taste, heaviness, judged intensity of electric shock" (Vincent, 1978, p. 232). Early psychophysical researchers had concluded that this relationship is governed by the formula $\psi = k(\phi - \phi_0)^n$. That is, "…the perceived magnitude ψ grows as the physical scale ϕ raised to a power $\underline{n}$. The ϕ_0 is often thought of as a threshold, while $\underline{k}$ is merely a constant that depends upon the units employed…. Most importantly, each of the modalities abiding by the law seems to have a characteristic exponent (n), ranging from 0.3 for brightness to 3.5 for apparent intensity of electric shock …" (Vincent, 1978, p. 232).

Psychophysical research, Vincent went on to explain, had expanded in the 1950s to include "stimuli that could be described only on a nominal (nonmetric) scale—attitudes, verbal statements, occupations, crimes, punishment, and musical selections, to name just a few…" (Vincent, 1978, p. 232). Where metrics could be scaled, the psychophysical power law seemed to hold. This led him to speculate that "[g]iven this background, it seemed worthwhile to bring the psychophysical tools to bear on the matter of scaling the difficulty of learning a foreign language" (Vincent, 1978, p. 232).

He proceeded to study Central Intelligence Agency Language School instructors' judgments (i.e., perceptions) of the difficulty of attaining any particular level of proficiency based on the FSI (now ILR) scale. The results, based on two differing techniques termed "magnitude estimation" and "ratio estimation," did indeed conform to the psychophysical power law, "[w]here ψ refers to estimated difficulty, $\underline{k}$ is a constant with a value of .01 or .03, depending on the psychophysical technique, ϕ is duration of training, ϕ_0 is a constant with a value of 37 for magnitude estimation and 0 for ratio estimation, and $\underline{n}$ = 1.00 for magnitude estimation and 1.03 for ratio estimation" (Vincent, 1978, p. 235). This equation itself, describing as it did proportionality between perceived and actual difficulty of L2 learning to particular proficiency levels, may be considered unremarkable from the point of view of L2 acquisition (finding, essentially, that experienced instructors are able to effectively estimate difficulty). What was eye-catching, however, was the light that this study cast on the almost logarithmic scale of actual difficulty, measured in training hours, when graphed against the FSI's ordinal scale of proficiency levels (viz., when graphed to yield equally spaced units along the x and y axes). Moreover, by demonstrating the proportionality between actual and perceived difficulty, Vincent was able to project his graph of difficulty out to FSI (ILR) Levels 4, 4+, 5, which were not represented in the available training data. Vincent described a number of limitations of his study, but the straightforward takeaway was that the amount of training time needed to move from any one proficiency level to the next appeared to increase logarithmically ("exponentially" as described by Lowe, 1985a, 1985b) as one ascended the proficiency ladder.

The actual term "inverted pyramid" and its employment as a visual depiction of the difficulty of attaining ever higher L2 proficiency levels originated with Ray Clifford in 1979 (Clifford, personal communication, October 24, 2019). The inverted pyramid appears to have been first presented visually by Clifford in a 1980 conference paper (cited here as Clifford, 1980; it does not appear to have been preserved).[54]

Clifford's 1980 representation was reproduced by Lowe, with slight differences, in two 1985 publications. Several features of the depiction in Figure 5 (from Lowe,

---

54 Clifford also presented at the 1978 conference at which Vincent presented his paper, the results of which formalized long-standing observations by USG language professionals concerning the course of L2 proficiency development.

1985a) are noteworthy. First, this pyramid is hexagonal, its six faces corresponding to the factors considered relevant to measuring oral proficiency in the USG context at that time. Second, what are explicitly depicted by this pyramid appear to be aspects of performance, rather than times to proficiency level. Third, the slope appears "exponential," rather than linear.[55]

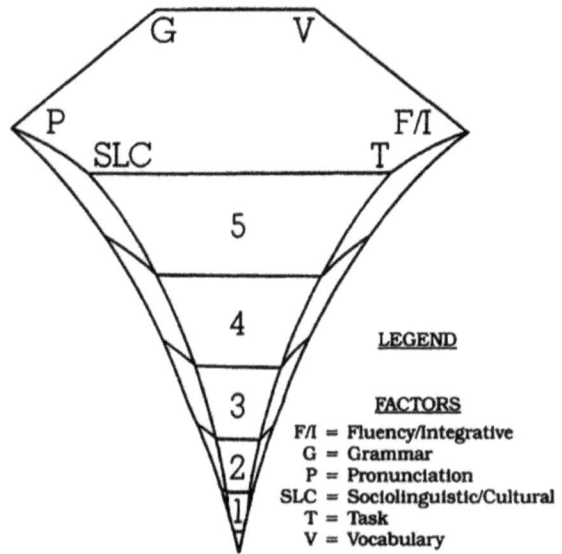

Ray T. Clifford. "Testing Oral Language Proficiency: A Dynamic Model." Paper presented at the Second Language Testing Symposium of the Interuniversitäre Sprachtestgruppe, Darmstadt, Germany, May 1980.

Fig. 5 (reproduced from Lowe, 1985a)

Figure 6 (Lowe, 1985b) shows development in two respects. First, it encloses the flaring ("exponential") slope of the pyramid in straight lines which connect Level 0 with the top of the Level 5 range. Clifford (personal communication, October 24, 2019) explains that the initial drawing was in fact linear, with the flaring shape added subsequently to reinforce the expanding nature of the scale, and that linear and flaring drawings coexisted for several years.[56] Second, Figure 6 encloses the lower ranges of proficiency (Levels 0–2+) in a box, evidently to indicate the partially compensatory nature of those lower levels in distinction to the non-compensatory nature of the upper levels of proficiency (ILR 3 and above).

---

55 Note that the differences in the pyramid's volume between successive levels increase (i.e., the difference between ILR 3 and 4 is greater than that between ILR 2 and 3, etc.) regardless of how we characterize the slope.

56 The ultimate "triumph" of the linear version may have resulted in part from a desire to deemphasize the exponential nature of the proficiency growth curve because of its potential impact on learner motivation. It is unlikely to have reflected researchers' uncertainty as to the objective contour of the L2 learning pyramid, as Lowe states in the same paper (Lowe, 1985b, 25, emphasis added) that "[a] complicating factor in discussing the scale is *its exponential growth, which Vincent ... established through a study in psychophysical scaling with Language School raters and which Clifford depicts graphically in his Inverted Pyramid...*"

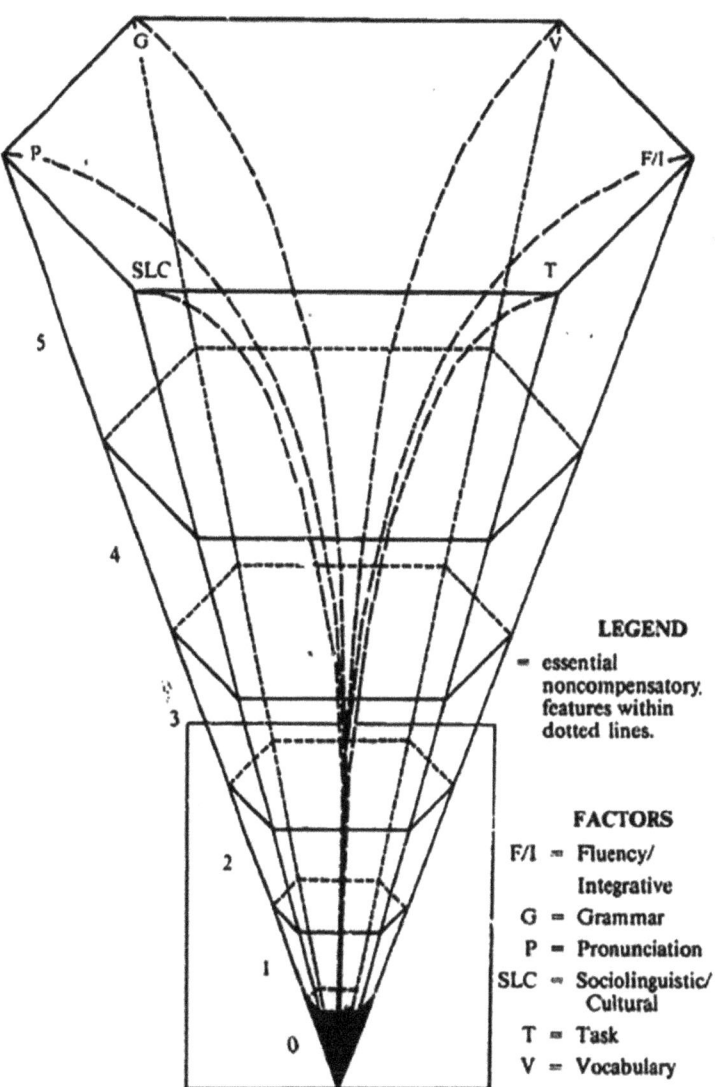

Fig. 6 (reproduced from Lowe, 1985b)

Clifford explains that subsequently, after references to the six "factors" were dropped, USG researchers moved to a two-dimensional linear "triangle" depiction that expressed the expanding nature of the scale more generally.

A preliminary depiction of the ACTFL inverted pyramid was also presented by Lowe (1985b, reproduced here as Figure 7). In it, the presumed exponential rate of proficiency development is de-emphasized in relation to the Figure 6. Lowe does not discuss the reason for this, but it may reflect the complementary USG (ILR: focus on upper ranges of proficiency) and academic (ACTFL: emphasis on lower ranges of proficiency) interests and realities (Halleck, 1990; Liskin-Gasparro, 1984; Lowe, 1983, 1985b), making the especially flaring shape toward the upper ranges of proficiency seem less important (and potentially demotivating to learners) in an academic context. The ACTFL inverted pyramid thus provided more granularity at the lower levels of proficiency, while the FSI/ILR inverted pyramid focused more on the upper ranges of proficiency. A further related difference between the two depictions was that the ACTFL scale originally indicated "Superior" as a ceiling, rather than a range.

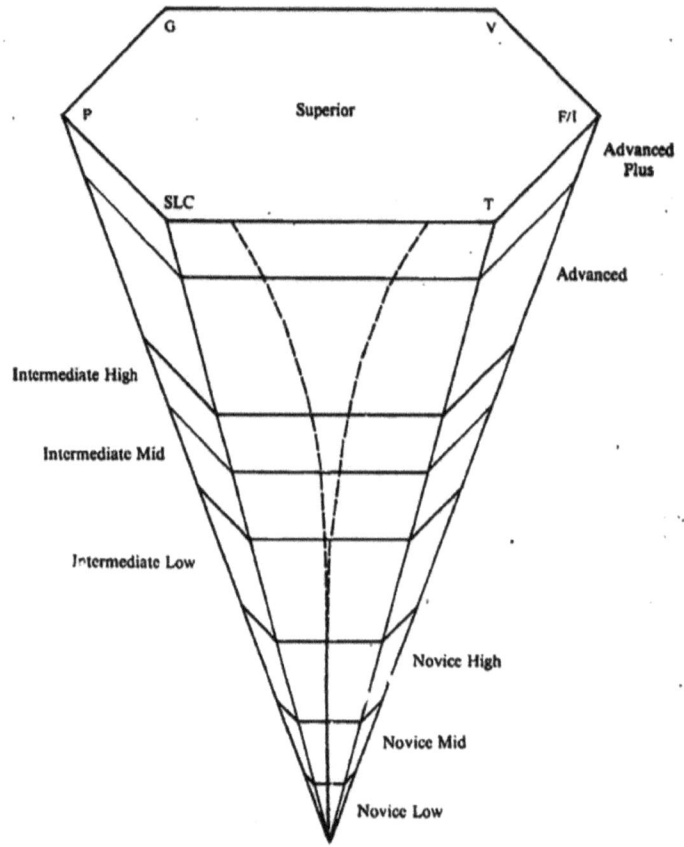

Fig. 7 (reproduced from Lowe, 1985b)

This brings us essentially up to the current ACTFL depiction of the inverted pyramid (Figure 8), through a number of graphically similar intermediate representations (for example, Liskin-Gasparro, 1984; Halleck, 1990). In the current ACTFL version, there is no longer any suggestion of a flaring (exponential) slope; the slope of the inverted pyramid's expansion is linear. This depiction also suggests a partial shift of focus toward the upper ranges of proficiency. "Distinguished" (corresponding to ILR Levels 4 and 5) has been included as a ceiling (not a range), while "Superior" is now a range, though still not divided into sub-levels.[57] A further innovation is that while the six faces of the inverted pyramid are retained, no significance for the six edges or faces is indicated. Lyons (2018), possibly in recognition of this circumstance, provides an equivalent drawing in the shape of an inverted cone.

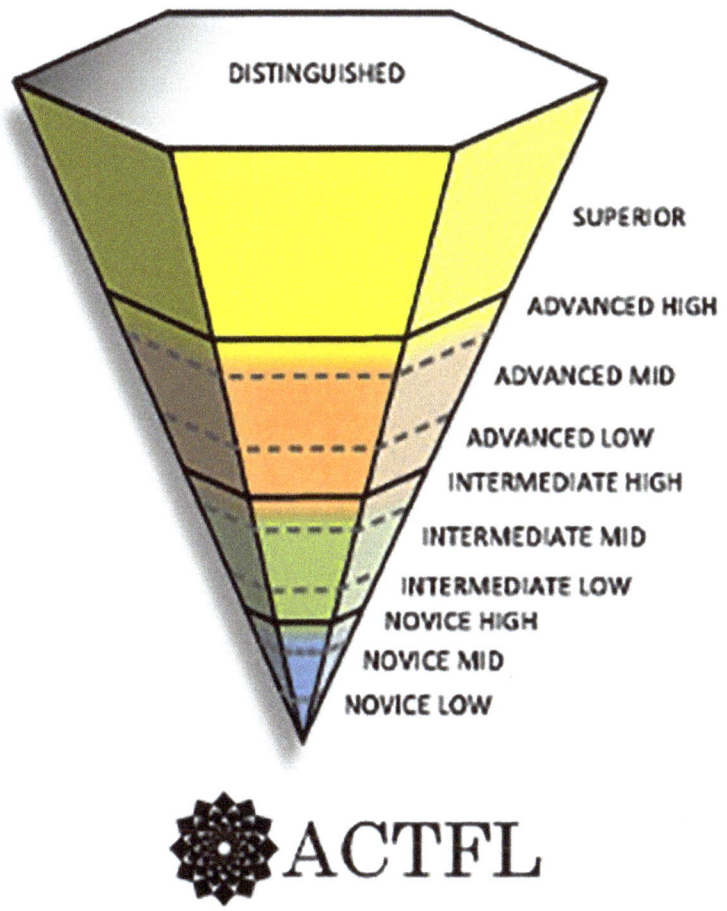

Fig. 8 (reproduced from the ACTFL website, with permission.)[58]

In 1983, Savignon proposed an inverted pyramid depiction of communicative competence that appears unrelated to the representation of proficiency levels proposed by Clifford which evolved into the ACTFL inverted pyramid. Savignon's pyramid, in its 2002 rendition (Figure 9), has three faces, one each for sociocultural,

---

57 This shift in focus is still only partial. In contrast to the ACTFL scale, the ILR recognizes "plus" levels 3+ and 4+. 3+ ratings are routinely awarded in USG training environments, while in my experience the awarding of 4+ has been considered problematic.

58 I am grateful to the American Council on the Teaching of Foreign Languages for permission to reproduce this figure.

discourse and grammatical competence. There is also an additional "vein" of strategic competence. As is readily discernible, Savignon's inverted pyramid of communicative competence has some similarities ("grammatical" and "sociocultural" faces) to Clifford's inverted pyramid of proficiency levels. There are also significant differences. Aside from the incomplete correspondence between the domains that are indicated, in Savignon's conception the intersecting dimension denotes expanding "contexts" in which learners possess communicative competence. In ACTFL and ILR depictions this dimension is unlabeled; we can surmise that initially it referred to quantity of learning required for each of the labeled factors contributing to proficiency. Overall, Savignon's depiction appears more closely related to the functional trisection approach to defining the components of oral proficiency toward which researchers were moving at about this same time (see the discussion below).

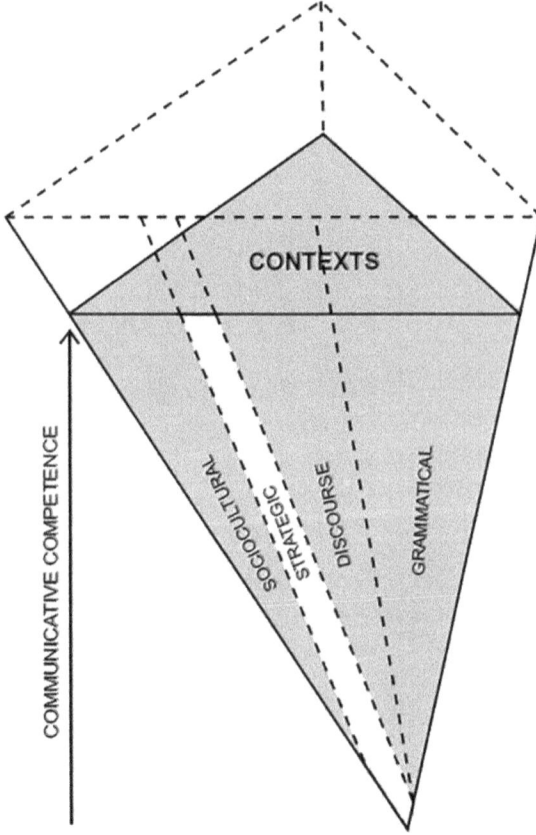

Fig. 9. Savignon's Model
Reproduced from Savignon, *Interpreting Communicative Language Teaching*, Yale University Press, copyright 2002.

One striking characteristic of Savignon's model concerns the non-expanding "vein" of strategic competence.[59] Within the communicative competence framework strategic competence refers to *communicative* strategies employed to compensate for lacunae in one's (or one's interlocutor's) linguistic proficiency. According to Savignon (1997, p. 46), "[b]eginning with the inverted tip of the pyramid and moving upward, grammatical, sociolinguistic, and discourse competence increase along with a corresponding overall increase in communicative competence. Strategic competence is present at all levels of proficiency although its importance in relation to the other components diminishes as knowledge of grammatical, sociolinguistic, and discourse rules increases."

In contrast, strategic competence here is conceived more broadly, to encompass both communicative and learning strategies (Ehrman, Leaver & Oxford, 2003; Leaver, Ehrman & Shekhtman, 2005), the latter typically reflecting at the outset of study native personality and cognitive/learning style variables. There is now a significant body of literature originating no later than the 1970s in regard to cognitive and learning style in general education with relevance to L2 learning, as well as literature specifically on strategic competence in L2 learning, which advocates a need for learners to develop what we might term "strategic maturity" or "strategic ambidexterity"—a broad range of strategies suited to diverse circumstances. This variegated strategic toolbox represents part of the equipment that becomes progressively more important as one approaches the ILR 3 (Superior) "base camp" and is indispensable during the ascent toward the (Distinguished-level) heights near the summit.

One takeaway from this historical review, aside from an understanding of the context in which it arose, is that although the inverted pyramid captures an apparent reality of critical importance in the quest for the summit—one which reflects generations of professional experience—it remains far from obvious how this reality can best be conceptualized and articulated. We will return to this question below in discussing the substance and shape of the inverted pyramid.

3.2. Does the Inverted Pyramid Exist?

Before turning to those questions, however, we must first validate whether this construct corresponds to any reality. In other words, is there really such a thing as an inverted pyramid of attainment of L2 proficiency levels? Numerous publications and handbooks from the 1980s onward (e.g., Reschke, 1984; Liskin-Gasparro, 1987; Defense Language Institute Foreign Language Center, 2010; and many others) have assumed the validity of the inverted pyramid construct, whether generally or in some particular form. Research addressing the validity of the construct, however,

---

[59] Strictly speaking, it expands in two dimensions rather than in three.

has been surprisingly limited.[60] Three types of studies have suggested some form of formal or informal validation.

The first consists of studies in connection with classroom instruction at learners' home institutions. The "instigational" role of Vincent (1978) has been discussed above. Meredith (1990) is framed as a follow-up to Lowe's challenge to view "the ILR proficiency scale as a synthesizing research principle" (Lowe, 1985b, p. 9). Toward that end, the author compared the statistical fit of five different scales as numerical correlates to the levels of the ACTFL proficiency scale using data obtained from OPIs of 127 first-year Spanish language students at Brigham Young University. Some of these students had previous experience with Spanish or other languages, which presumably explains the fact that results were obtained at all levels up to but not including Superior. Meredith concluded that scales which had progressively greater distance as one "climbed" the proficiency ladder fit the data better than a purely nominal 0-10 scale (1 = Novice-Low, 10 = Superior). A secondary source confirming some form of inverted pyramid is provided by Liskin-Gasparro (1984, 478), which cites an apparently unpublished FSI document: "Data from the FSI indicate that it takes 240 hours of instruction for a professional adult with average language-learning aptitude to reach Level 1 in a language that is relatively close to English, such as French, Italian, or Spanish. To move to Level 2 requires 480 hours; even after 720 hours, proficiency no higher than Level 2+ can be expected."

None of the studies cited above is less than 30 years old. This needs to be borne in mind in considering what will be said below about the possible influence of instructional approaches on the inverted pyramid phenomenon.

Other studies bearing on validation concern proficiency gain during study abroad programs. Brecht, Davidson, and Ginsberg (1993, p. 17) noted that "[o]n all modalities [i.e., listening, reading, and speaking] the higher the initial level, the less likely a gain." The authors interpreted this result in terms of an s-shaped learning curve, rather than an inverted pyramid. Further on, though, they seem to imply that they were assuming an inverted pyramid in regard to attaining proficiency (Level 2, specifically): "… if one takes the often quoted Foreign Service Institute scale concerning the amount of time required to learn Level 3 and 4 languages as a basis, assuming five hours a week of instruction in a college course, it would take eight years to equal the amount of instruction required by the FSI to produce a Level 2 speaker in Russian" (18). Davidson and Shaw (2019) generally support the conclusion of Brecht, Davidson, and Ginsberg (1993). There is an important "twist," however, that we will describe below regarding the shape of the inverted pyramid.

A number of further studies may be viewed as indirectly suggestive of an inverted pyramid by showing that even among undergraduate language majors few attain ILR 3 (Superior) or higher during a four-year degree program: Carroll (1967); Mag-

---

60 See Tigchelaar (2019) for one recent overview.

nan (1986); Swender (2003); Rifkin (2005); Tschirner (2011, 2016); Winke, Gass, and Heidrich (2019), among others.

Language Testing International (2020, which cites as its source Liskin-Gasparro, 1982)[61] gives expected proficiency levels typically achieved after 8, 16, 24 and 44 weeks of study for languages of Category 1 (e.g., French and Spanish among the "commonly taught" languages) through Category 4. This chart shows the level at which students typically find themselves in specified weeks of study rather than numbers of weeks required to *attain* particular levels, which limits its significance for the questions raised here. It appears to be suggestive of an exponential inverted pyramid though it encompasses three comparable base levels (Intermediate Low, Advanced Low and Superior) only for Category 4 languages (e.g., Arabic, Chinese, Japanese, Korean) for learners with "average" aptitude, with no indication (other than a reference to the source) as to how measurements (including aptitude) were taken.

There has also been a limited literature (now largely dated) that has questioned the inverted pyramid concept (Lantolf & Frawley, 1985).

The literature to date thus suggests that the inverted pyramid construct does capture a reality of L2 learning and is thus a factor of significance for the attainment of Distinguished-level proficiency. It provides insufficient answers, however, and in some cases no answer, to the more detailed questions whose answers could assist us in meeting the challenge:

- What is its shape—how many faces and edges does it have; are they symmetrical?
- What is its slope, and is that slope (including any acceleration) constant?
- Does it exist (or does it exist in the same shape) for all learners, or for all L1–L2 pairs?
- Does it manifest itself in all learning environments, or is it an artifact (at least in part) of particular instructional and curricular approaches?

Then there are methodological questions such as:

- Can one measure time-to-next-proficiency-level with any more precision than through end-of-course testing?
- How does one quantify learning time? Should one look at calendar time, course hours, actual time-on-task? Should one take into consideration gaps between courses, intensity of study (e.g., taking multiple courses vs. just one course per term, 5 day per week courses differently from 3 day per week courses with the same class hours),

---

61   I have not been able to consult Liskin-Gasparro (1982).

in-country class activities differently from home institution activities? Should we factor in out-of-class learning-related activities (e.g., homework or personal initiative), and should we do this differently for study abroad?

The answers to these questions are by no means obvious. For example, Leaver (Coalition of Distinguished Language Centers, 2008; Leaver, 2013) has drawn a distinction between "tortoises" and "hares"[62] that casts doubt on the universal applicability of the inverted pyramid construct to all learners. "Hares" (typically synoptic learners,[63] earlier termed "right-brain dominant") initially acquire language quickly but tend early on to become "awfully fluent" and to be subject to fossilization and to plateauing around ILR 2+ – 3. "Tortoises" (typically ectenic learners,[64] earlier termed "left-brain dominant") begin slowly and may struggle initially, may be "painfully ac¬curate" early on, and may plateau around ILR 1+ – 2 but "take off" at later stages of study.[65]

Davidson and Shaw's findings (2019, discussed below) suggest that the slope of the inverted pyramid could be reversed between the Advanced and Superior level for some learner cohorts. Rifkin (2005) argues that intensity of L2 engagement can be a "force multiplier." We will examine some of these questions in the following sections.

3.3. What is the Inverted Pyramid?

Let us now consider whether we can characterize the inverted pyramid with greater precision. First and foremost, what is the stuff of the inverted pyramid, i.e., what is it a pyramid of? Two general conceptions have been available and have been evoked since its origin, not necessarily as an intentional distinction. According to one, this pyramid depicts an expanding quantity of learning, however we choose to define and articulate it, that must be achieved to attain ever higher levels of proficiency. According to the other, it depicts the expanding quantity of time that is required for the same purpose. The early depictions published by Lowe for both the

---

62 The early grounding of this distinction can be found in Leaver (1986), with exemplification from FSI experience in Leaver and Corin (2019) and classroom applications in Coalition of Distinguished Language Centers (2008).

63 Synoptic learners are defined by Ehrman and Leaver (2003) as those who learn unconsciously or osmotically.

64 Ectenic learners are defined by Ehrman and Leaver (2003) as those who learn consciously and deliberatively.

65 Levels at which plateauing typically occur are based on Leaver (1986), which determined "hemispheric dominance" through a learning styles questionnaire (Torrance et al. 1977). This terminology was later supplanted by the "synoptic—ectenic" distinction to avoid confusion of hemispheric dominance as a learning styles metaphor with the marginally parallel biological reality of hemispheric differences in information processing (Leaver, personal communication, December 25, 2020).

ILR and ACTFL scales (described above) are labeled to suggest the former interpretation. The straightforward and natural assumption would be that an expanding quantity of learning is giving rise to an expanding time-to-next-proficiency-level. Vincent (1978) studies time-to-proficiency-level as an indicator of "difficulty," which seems to imply such a conception. The current ACTFL inverted pyramid is unspecified in this regard.

Yet it is not obvious that the "learning quantity $\propto$ time quantity"[66] interpretation of the inverted pyramid is accurate, or that it reflects, to some extent, an inherent and immutable reality of L2 learning. While the "time-to-next-proficiency-level" interpretation reflects the observations of many L2 professionals and some research, validation of its relation to "quantity of learning" depends on articulating just what this learning is and how much there is of it, both in terms of categories and of specific content.

Viewing the first part of this question (defining the most salient components, factors or performance domains contributing to proficiency) in terms of the inverted pyramid, this would come down to specifying the number of its edges or faces and what each signifies. The answers may vary from skill to skill. Clifford's 1980 depiction operated with six factors contributing to oral proficiency, though he and others questioned whether this was in fact the optimal articulation of contributing factors (Lowe, 1985b). At around this same time or shortly after, researchers were shifting to the conception of a functional trisection of oral proficiency comprised of "functions," "content" and "accuracy" (Higgs & Clifford, 1982)[67] or a quintasection of reading proficiency (Lowe, 1985b).[68] Savignon's inverted pyramid depicts five factors in two planes, perhaps closer to the functional trisection approach. As of 2010, the ILR approach to oral proficiency testing operated with a functional quatrosection (Defense Language Institute Foreign Language Center, 2010), reflecting the addition of text type to the trisection. Other researchers (e.g., Iwashita, 2010; De Jong et al., 2012), have proposed different articulations at least of factors significant for *measuring* oral proficiency.

In regard to the second part of the question, that of quantifying the components of proficiency, however we choose to articulate proficiency and whatever units of measure we define, this also brings us to the question of how to define the nature of the intersecting plane, which versions to date of the inverted pyramid have depicted as parallel with the ceiling of the pyramid? What does this plane signify (e.g., contexts, as in Savignon's inverted pyramid), and how is it measured?

The previous two questions, in turn, lead us to that of the regularity (symmetry) of the pyramid's shape. For example, should the distances between levels at

---

66 $\propto$ = "proportional to."

67 This trisection is analogous to the three facets of criterion-referenced assessment (Clifford, 2016).

68 I leave out of account here, on account of space, the substantive question of whether there is a distinct inverted pyramid for each skill (speaking, reading, listening, writing), concerning which a considerable body of research and experience exists.

each edge be identical, so that the floors or ceilings of each proficiency level all appear flat and lay parallel to one another? That is how the inverted pyramid has been depicted to date but does not conform to any consensus among researchers. While numerous studies examine the development of individual components of proficiency, I am not aware of studies that attempt to quantify this purported expanding quantity of learning synthetically across a full range of relevant factors, dimensions or domains of competency or performance in a manner that is relatable to the inverted pyramid construct. Higgs and Clifford (1982), while not attempting to model absolute measures (quantities) for any component of proficiency, did propose a hypothetical model of the varying relative significance of five linguistic factors in achieving successive levels of oral proficiency (see Figure 10). Attempting to incorporate their hypothesis into graphic representations of the inverted pyramid would be tricky, to say the least. A number of more recent studies have attempted to test or reproduce this finding, typically based, however, on differing conceptions of the components of proficiency to be measured (e.g., Iwashita, 2010; De Jong et al., 2012 with their literature reviews), reaching differing conclusions that are not fully comparable. The questions of absolute measures of learning and relative measures of participation in proficiency at any particular level are by no means insignificant matters, as issues of focus, learner counseling and resource allocation in curriculum and program development can flow from the answer.

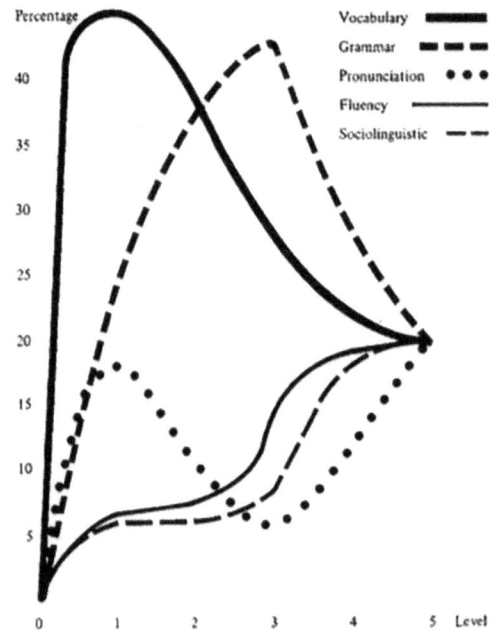

Fig. 10 (reproduced from Higgs & Clifford, 1982)

The most obvious question—that which provided the impetus for the creation of the inverted pyramid—concerns its slope: *how much* more difficult is it to attain each successive proficiency level, or how much more time does it require? This question, whether we define it in terms of the inverted pyramid metaphor or not, is a critical matter with obvious implications for strategic, program, and curricular planning as well as resource allocation.

As described above, the limited available research and non-systematic observations have suggested an "exponential" curve, to use Lowe's phrase, but are by no means conclusive. Vincent was acutely aware of the limitations of his initial study; the exponential nature of the curve appeared to be strongly supported, but he was less confident of his specific numerical results and recognized the limits of the context within which they had been attained. Meredith's (1990) results also supported an exponential slope but appear not to have been followed up. Davidson and Shaw (2019, p. 223) state that "[a] more nuanced mathematical model has yet to be developed and accepted within the foreign language assessment community to account statistically for the time-on-task differentials implicit in the successive levels of the ILR proficiency scale."

It is at present little more than an assumption, moreover, that the slope of the inverted pyramid, including the acceleration (i.e., flaring, if any) of the slope, remains constant. One could conceive of entirely different shapes, for example one that first expands and then contracts. The results of Davidson and Shaw (2019) suggest that this latter possibility—expanding time-to-next-level between Levels 0 and 2, then decreasing time-to-next-level between Levels 2 and 3—is plausible, depending on program parameters and the context in which learning occurs. In their study, the authors examined proficiency gain (delta) of 308 U.S. secondary and university-level participants in year-long federally funded overseas immersion programs for Arabic, Chinese and Russian at incoming levels from Novice to Advanced. When measured on an ordinal 18-point scale of proficiency keyed to the levels of the ACTFL scale (2019, p. 224), they found that "[m]ean delta (OPI) was 5.81 for novice participants, 4.36 for intermediate participants, and 4.19 for advanced participants; gains in units of pre-program standard deviation were 7.30 for novice participants, 5.58 for intermediate participants, and 7.74 for advanced participants. Proficiency gains were comparable across levels, with gains at the intermediate level slightly more modest than those posted by the novices and advanced students" (2019, 232).

Davidson and Shaw related these findings to the "presumed cognitive, academic, and socio-emotional effects of the immersion intervention at more advanced levels of acquisition on the learning process" (p. 232). Foreshadowing the discussion in Sections 3.4. and 3.5., and considering these results in light of descriptions of the Language Flagship Capstone year abroad programs (e.g., Davidson, Garas, & Lekic, 2021), it furthermore seems likely that the approaches to learning utilized in the advanced-level study abroad programs examined shared substantial characteristics with the type of open architecture curricular model that, according to our hypothesis, should be useful in overcoming the inverted pyramid phenomenon.

Seen more broadly, these results may also suggest that at the point at which time-to-next-level tended to contract (between ILR 2 and 3) for these students, readiness to attain the next proficiency level may have been offsetting the actual difficulty of attaining that level. In other words, the learner attempting to move from Advanced to Superior may no longer be the same learner who previously attempted to move from Novice to Intermediate and on to Advanced. This conception would presumably view these more advanced learners as possessing an expanded learning capacity in multiple respects: expanded learning strategy arsenals or "strategic ambidexterity," including both preferred strategies and those typical of learners with opposite "native" learning styles; expanded sociocultural awareness, competencies and permeability, and so on. Such an effect, and the degree to which it is manifested, would of course depend in part on instructional practices and curricular design at earlier stages of study. Overall, these results as described by Davidson and Shaw support the view (recalling also Clifford's bucket analogy) that there may be no direct and inevitable correlation between the two senses of the inverted pyramid; that is, time-to-next-proficiency-level may not be inexorably proportional to the amount of learning that separates each level from the next. Returning to Lowe's mountain metaphor, this interpretation supports the need for learners aspiring to Distinguished-level proficiency to approach the base camp with the equipment needed for the ascent to the summit already in place.

The discussion to this point reinforces our recognition that it is an assumption (i.e., neither obvious nor established through research) that the inverted pyramid is a universal of L2 learning. To the contrary, it seems not only possible but probable that it depends in part on individual learner variables (e.g., the tortoises vs. hares phenomenon) as well as on instructional/curricular approaches, including the development of strategic ambidexterity (or style-flex, as Leaver has also termed this) and the form of OACD under consideration here. It is equally unclear whether the inverted pyramid is universally identical in substance and shape regardless of the specific L1–L2 pairing.

3.4. What Causes the Inverted Pyramid?

In lieu of a traditional concluding section, in the final two subsections let us summarize the discussion about the causes of the inverted pyramid phenomenon and avenues available to mitigate it.

As to what causes the inverted pyramid, four general answers have presented themselves, which are not mutually exclusive. The first, in line with commonly held perceptions, is that an ever-greater quantity of learning (however articulated and measured) must be accomplished to proceed through successive levels of proficiency. The second holds that the progressively less compensatory nature of higher levels of proficiency may play a role. Assuming their validity, these would be areas in which possibilities for treatment to counteract the inverted pyramid are inevitably limited. Nevertheless, the first is amenable to substantial mitigation by ensuring that every level's "bucket" is being filled simultaneously, which is a central thesis of this paper.

A third answer would be that learner variables play a role (implying significance for cohort variables as well). This would encompass a variety of readiness for learning issues, some of which may be ephemeral, others stable over time (e.g., Achterberg, 1988). Cognitive and learning style likely play a central role, and it is possible that learners with different individual profiles may tend toward entirely differently shaped "inverted pyramids." For some learners, the curve of progression from one proficiency level to the next may not look like an inverted pyramid at all. To use Leaver's metaphors, "hares" may have an exaggerated inverted pyramid, while "tortoises" may have no inverted pyramid at all, perhaps even a progression more akin to a non-inverted pyramid or a shape that first expands, then contracts like the facets of a diamond.

A fourth answer, linked in an obvious way to the involvement of learner variables, is that instructional and curricular approaches may play a role in reinforcing or mitigating the inverted pyramid phenomenon. In regard to instruction, contributing factors could include instructors' (in)sufficient awareness of differences between learning requirements for lower and higher levels of proficiency. It is especially important that they assist learners to prepare for higher-level learning—to approach the base camp already possessing the equipment for the trek to the summit. If the instructional approach allows fossilization of patterned error or strategic fossilization to develop, the ability of learners to move beyond (or even to attain) ILR 3 (Superior) will be diminished and the required time presumably greatly increased. As for curricular design choices, linear scope and sequence, which creates a non-inverted pyramid of exposure to and time-on-task with ever higher-level text and task types and their associated linguistic/paralinguistic elements, would be predicted to contribute to an inverted pyramid effect.

3.5. What Can We Do about the Inverted Pyramid?

Finally, what are the paths forward that our discussion of the inverted pyramid suggests to us? This will bring us full circle, back to the hypothesis proposed in Section 2 about the effect of modular vertically spiraled OACD on the inverted pyramid phenomenon.

Based on all that has been noted above, at least two general approaches are available to mitigate, counteract, eliminate or avoid the inverted pyramid, as well as a variety of specific treatments based on them, either individually or, preferably, in combination. One approach is related to instruction, the other to curriculum.

In regard to instruction, the way forward is fairly clear, and involves many of the best practices for L2 learning that have been emerging in recent years. One of the most important involves employing *diagnostic instruction* at all proficiency levels: incorporating awareness of learner and cohort individuality and learners' current zone of proximal development, adapting to them and seizing opportunities as they arise based on ongoing formative assessment. This requires that we leverage personality factors, cognitive style, sensory preferences, motivational profile, educational and biographical background in addition to learners' ever-changing linguistic profiles. Treating learning style factors through both accommodational and confrontational (e.g., strategy-building) approaches is critical—systematically programing strategy building into the instructional process to create strategic ambidexterity: hare-like tortoises and tortoise-like hares. Ensuring early awareness of, and gradual adaptation to, requirements of learning that will take on greater importance as one approaches higher proficiency levels (e.g., accuracy and sociocultural competencies) is also critical, building these gradually from Day 1 to avoid a "wall of fossilization"—both linguistic and strategic—near ILR 2 (Advanced) for some learners.

Alongside managing learner and cohort individuality, other major areas of (by now largely established) best practice to defeat the inverted pyramid involve:

- integration into the learning process from Day 1, and reliance on, authentic target language texts, maximizing their use throughout the course of learning and adapting, as necessary, the task to the text rather than the text to the task;

- engagement of critical reflection and higher-order thinking through task-, scenario-, project- and content-based learning and immersive (TL-only) environment from Day 1 of learning.

These approaches would be predicted to (and appear in fact to) mitigate the non-inverted pyramid of exposure to and time-on-task with ever higher-level text and task types that we posit to be one of the causal factors of the inverted pyramid.

In order to ensure that these instructional desiderata can be enabled to maximal effect, however, choices in regard to curricular design are critical. One obvious way to incorporate these approaches systematically into curricular design is to transition to open architecture curriculum based on vertical spiraling at the earliest possible stage of learning. The modular SBL and SBL-CBL OACD designs illustrated in this article (and described in greater detail in previous publications) were designed in part to accomplish these goals. One of the most significant discoveries has been that in a conversion environment vertically spiraled OACD from Day 1 of training can yield outcomes that appear remarkable in light of typical times needed to attain particular proficiency outcomes. This, in turn, suggests the desirability of pre-training and early training techniques to create "simulated conversion learners" who can engage in vertically spiraled OACD from the earliest possible date. A number of such pre-training techniques for some languages have been developed and tested at small scale over the years but have not yet become a mainstream trend in L2 learning.

Acknowledgements

The author is grateful to the following organizations for permission to reproduce graphics used in this article: American Council on Teaching Foreign Language (along with Wiley & Sons), Cambridge University Press, and Yale University Press. Attributions appear on the appropriate graphics.

References

Achterberg, C. (1988). Factors that influence learner readiness. *Journal of the American Dietetic Association 88*(11): 1426-1428.

ACTFL (American Council on the Teaching of Foreign Languages). *General preface to the ACTFL Proficiency Guidelines 2012.* Downloaded from https://www.actfl.org/publications/guidelines-and-manuals/actfl-proficiency-guidelines-2012

Brecht, R. D., Davidson, D., & Ginsberg, R. B. (1993). *Predictors of foreign language gain during study abroad.* Washington, D.C.: The National Foreign Language Center.

Campbell, C. (2021). Open Architecture Curricular Design: A fundamental principle of transformative language learning and teaching. In B. L. Leaver, D. E. Davidson, & C. Campbell (Eds.), *Transformative language learning and teaching* (pp. 43-50). Cambridge, UK: Cambridge University Press.

Campbell, C., Corin, A. R., Kanbar, H., & Leaver, B. L. (2017). Pushing the envelope: Transformative pedagogy in outcomes-based foreign language instruction. *University of California, Los Angeles. Tenth International Conference on Language Teacher Education.* Los Angeles.

Carroll, J. B. (1967). *The foreign language attainments of language majors in the senior year: A survey conducted in U.S. colleges and universities.* Cambridge, MA: Harvard University.

Clifford, R. T. (1980). Testing oral language proficiency: A dynamic model. *Second Language Testing Symposium of the Interuniversitäre Sprachtestgruppe.* Darmstadt, Germany.

Clifford, R. (2016). A rationale for criterion-referenced proficiency testing. *Foreign Language Annals 49*(2): 224-234.

Coalition of Distinguished Language Centers. (2008). *What works: Helping students reach native-like second-language competence.* Salinas, CA: MSI Press.

Corin, A. (1997). A course to convert Czech proficiency to proficiency in Croatian and Serbian. In S. B. Stryker & B. L. Leaver (Eds.), *Content-based instruction in foreign language education: Models and methods* (pp. 78-104). Washington, D.C.: Georgetown University Press.

Corin, A. R. (2020a). Open architecture curriculum and transformative language learning revisited. Part 1. The relationship between open architecture curricular design and transformative language learning. *ACTR Letter 46*(3-4): 1-2, 4-5.

Corin, A. R. (2020b). Open architecture curriculum and transformative language learning revisited. Part 2. Toward a constrained definition of OACD. *ACTR Letter 47*(1): 1-2, 4.

Corin, A. R. (2021). Foreign language learning efficiency: Transformative learning in an outcomes-based environment. In B. L. Leaver, D. E. Davidson, & C. Campbell (Eds.), *Transformative language learning and teaching* (pp. 51-60). Cambridge, UK: Cambridge University Press.

Dababneh, R. (2018). The scenario-based syllabus for the post-basic Arabic program at the DLIFLC. *Dialog on Language Instruction 28*(1): 13-26.

Davidson, D. E., Garas, N., & Lekic, M. D. (2021). Transformative language learning in the overseas immersion environment: Exploring affordances of intercultural development. In B. L. Leaver, D. E. Davidson, & C. Campbell (Eds.), *Transformative language learning and teaching* (pp. 107-119). Cambridge, UK: Cambridge University Press.

Davidson, D. E., & Shaw, J. R. (2019). A cross-linguistic and cross-skill perspective on L2 development in study abroad. In P. Winke & S. M. Gass (Eds.), *Foreign language proficiency in higher education* (pp. 217-242). Cham, Switzerland: Springer.

Defense Language Institute Foreign Language Center. (2010). *OPI tester certification workshop training manual.* Monterey, CA: Defense Language Institute Foreign Language Center Evaluation and Standardization Directorate, Proficiency Standards Division.

De Jong, N. H., Steinel, M. P., Florijn, A. F., Schoonen, R., & Hulstijn, J. H. (2012). Facets of speaking proficiency. *Studies in Second Language Acquisition 34*: 5-34.

Derderian, A. (2017). Designing for teaching and learning in an open world: Task supported open architecture language instruction. *International Journal of Adult Vocational Education and Technology 8*(3): 55-67.

Ehrman, M. E., & Leaver, B. L. (2003). Cognitive styles in the service of language learning. *System 31*(3): 393-415.

Ehrman, M. E., Leaver, B. L., & Oxford, R. L. (2003). A brief overview of individual differences in second language learning. *System 31*(3): 313-330.

Halleck, G. B. (1990). *Assessing the oral proficiency of Chinese speakers of English as a foreign language: Holistic rating versus the objective measure of syntactic maturity.* Doctoral dissertation. University Park, PA: The Pennsylvania State University.

Higgs, T. V., & Clifford, R. (1982). The push toward communication. In T. V. Higgs (Ed.), *Curriculum, competence, and the foreign language teacher (pp 57-79).* Lincolnwood, IL: National Textbook Company.

Iwashita, N. (2010). Features of oral proficiency in task performance by EFL and JFL learners. In M. T. Prior, Y. Watanabe, & S.-K. Lee (Eds.), *Selected proceedings of the 2008 Second Language Research Forum* (pp. 32-47). Somerville, MA: Cascadilla Press, Proceedings Project.

Krasner, I. (2018). Open architecture approach to teaching Russian as a foreign language. *ACTR Letter 45*(2): 1-2, 4-5.

Language Testing International. (2020). *How long does it take to become proficient?* Downloaded from https://www.languagetesting.com/how-long-does-it-take

Lantolf, J. P., & Frawley, W. (1985). Oral proficiency testing: A critical analysis. *The Modern Language Journal 69*: 337-345.

Leaver, B. L. (1986). Hemisphericity of the brain and foreign language teaching. *Folia Slavica 8*: 76-90.

Leaver, B. L. (2013). *Achieving native-like second language proficiency: A catalogue of critical factors, Volume 1: Speaking.* Virginia Beach, VA: Virginia Institute Press.

Leaver, B. L., & Corin, A. R. (2019). Fields of the mind: An integral learning styles component of the E&L Cognitive Styles Construct. *Russian Language Journal 69*: 61-87.

Leaver, B. L., Ehrman, M., & Shekhtman, B. (2005). *Achieving success in second language acquisition.* Cambridge, MA: Cambridge University Press.

Liskin-Gasparro, J. E. (1982). *ETS oral proficiency testing manual.* Princeton, NJ: Educational Testing Service.

Liskin-Gasparro, J. E. (1984). The ACTFL Proficiency Guidelines: Gateway to testing and curriculum. *Foreign Language Annals 17*(5): 475-489.

Liskin-Gasparro, J. E. (1987). *Testing and teaching for oral proficiency.* Boston: Heinle.

Lowe, P., Jr. (1983). The ILR oral interview: Origins, applications, pitfalls, and implications. *Die Unterrichtspraxis/Teaching German 16*(2): 230-244.

Lowe, P., Jr. (1985a). Proficiency-based curriculum design: Principles derived from government experience. *Die Unterrichtspraxis/Teaching German 18*(2): 233-245.

Lowe, P., Jr. (1985b). The ILR proficiency scale as a synthesizing research principle: The view from the mountain. In C. J. James (Ed.), *Foreign language proficiency in the classroom and beyond* (pp. 9-54). Lincolnwood, IL: National Textbook Company.

Lyons, D. (2018). How (and why) to determine your level of language proficiency. *Babbel Magazine.* https://www.babbel.com/en/magazine/how-and-why-to-determine-language-proficiency

Magnan, S. S. (1986). Assessing speaking proficiency in the undergraduate curriculum: Data from French. *Foreign Language Annals 19*(5): 429-438.

Meredith, R. A. (1990). The oral proficiency interview in real life: Sharpening the scale. *The Modern Language Journal 74*(3): 288-296.

Reschke, C. (1984). Oral proficiency testing: Meeting a variety of needs. *Die Unterrichtspraxis/Teaching German 17*(2): 265-278.

Rifkin, B. (2005). A ceiling effect in traditional classroom foreign language instruction: Data from Russian. *The Modern Language Journal 89*(1): 3-18.

Savignon, S. J. (1997). *Communicative competence: Theory and classroom practice* (2nd ed.). New York: McGraw-Hill.

Savignon, S. J. (2002). Communicative language teaching: Linguistic theory and classroom practice. In S. J. Savignon (Ed.), *Interpreting communicative language teaching: Contexts and concerns in teacher education* (pp. 1-27). New Haven, CT: Yale University Press.

School of Language Studies. (1986). *Bridges.* Arlington, VA: U.S. Department of State, Foreign Service Institute.

Stevick, E. W. (1971). *Adapting and writing language lessons.* Arlington, VA: U.S. Department of State, Foreign Service Institute.

Swender, E. (2003). Oral proficiency testing in the real world: Answers to frequently asked questions. *Foreign Language Annals 36*(4): 520-526.

Tarone, E. (2017). Exploring learner language in language teacher education. *University of California, Los Angeles. Tenth International Conference on Language Teacher Education.* Los Angeles.

Tigchelaar, M. (2019). Exploring the relationship between self-assessments and OPIc ratings of oral proficiency in French. In P. Winke & S. M. Gass (Eds.), *Foreign language proficiency in higher education* (pp. 153-173). Cham, Switzerland: Springer.

Torrance, E. P., Reynolds, C. R., Riegel, T., & Ball, O. E. (1977). Your style of learning and thinking, forms A and B: Preliminary norms abbreviated technical scores scoring keys, and selected references. *Gifted Child Quarterly 21*: 563-573.

Tschirner, E. (2011). Reasonable expectations: Frameworks of reference, proficiency levels, educational standards. *Studie z aplikované lingvistiky/Studies in Applied Linguistics 2011*(1), 101-119.

Tschirner, E. (2016). Listening and reading proficiency levels of college students. *Foreign Language Annals 49*(2): 201-223.

Vincent, R. J. (1978). Psychophysical scaling of the language proficiency interview: A preliminary report. In J. L. D. Clark (Ed.), *Direct testing of speaking proficiency: Theory and application* (pp. 229-253). Princeton, NJ: Educational Testing Service.

Winke, P., Gass, S. M., & Heidrich, E. S. (2019). Modern-day foreign language majors: Their goals, attainment, and fit within a twenty-first century curriculum. In P. Winke & S. M. Gass (Eds.), *Foreign language proficiency in higher education* (pp. 93-113). Cham, Switzerland: Springer.

Feature Article Contributors

Jennifer Bown
Professor of Russian
Brigham Young University

Tony Brown
Professor of Russian
Brigham Young University

Christine Campbell
Professor Emerita
Defense Language Institute Foreign Language Center

Andrew Corin
Professor Emeritus
Defense Language Institute Foreign Language Center

Mary Jo DiBiase-Lubrano
Associate Director
Center for Language Study
Yale University

Katya Jordan
Assistant Professor
Brigham Young University

Elizaveta Kurganova
Head of the Department of Russian as a Foreign Language
Institute for Social Sciences
Russian Presidential Academy of National Economy and Public Administration (RANEPA)

Betty Lou Leaver
Provost, retired
Defense Language Institute Foreign Language Center

Jana Vasilj-Begovic
Foreign Language Standards Officer
Department of National Defense of Canada

ABSTRACTS

Abstracts in Arabic
Amer Farraj

Our software does not process Arabic—yet.

Abstracts in Arabic may be found at www.msipress.com/journal-for-distinguished-language-studies/

Abstracts in Chinese
Yalun Zhou, Ph.D.

回顾过去，展望未来："四级外语水平运动"的历史

本文从历史的角度回顾了被称为四级外语水平运动的历程。该运动从八十年代中期开始，在2010年左右取得了辉煌的成就，然后在接下来的十年里缓慢下来，现在又重新在一小群富有经验和感兴趣的教师、学习者、和管理者中活跃起来。该运动的所有社会机制：年会、年会论文集、发表在与杰出语言中心联盟(CDLC)合作出版的国际刊物《杰出语言研究期刊》中的年度文章，等等，都随着2010年CDLC的关闭而停止了。当我们"展望"未来时，本文作者认为凤凰可以涅槃，并指出那些星火仍然还在继续燃烧的地方以及那些继续煽动火焰燃烧的个体。作者同时还提供了2010-2020年间出版的致力于四级外语水平运动的作品的概述。

Keywords 关键词: 优异级外语水平, 四级外语水平运动的历史, 杰出语言中心联盟, 杰出语言研究期刊, 四级外语水平出版物

重新思考评分过程：界定语言表达能力是否达标时测试难题的解决方案

测试的可靠性和有效性从本质上来说与评分标准息息相关。特别是在超高级语言水平能力作答题的测评中，评分者的培训水平和对测试标准的理解，以及他们对所有可能的正确答案的预见性至关重要。这些问题与测试标准的设置方法有关，这种标准的设置旨在建立两种被测评者的级别：达到或未达到语言表现的最低标准，从而印证作答题的设置和测试目的。本文描述了综合阅读理解测试中如何确定作答题的及格分数。这种确定方法叫混合性确定法，及把评分者的整体评分与单项评分综合考虑。这种方法，作者们称之为追溯性模型法 (Retrodictive Medeling Approach "RMA")。RMA 依靠评分者的专业水平和整体评分，加上定性分析和得分，从而产生一个分值来判断应试者的语言表现是否达到最低标准。尽管宣称本方法的通用性超出了本研究的范畴，但进一步的研究可能会让RMA在优异级语言水平能力测试中得到广泛应用。

关键词 Keywords: 标准设置、测试常态、评分有效性、优异级语言能力水平

重新定义语言课程以达到四级水平

由于对语言能力所要求的深度和广度，取得目标语四级水平对学习者来说是一个巨大的挑战。教学单位可以采取行之有效的措施，重新定义他们的语言课程以达到四级水平。这些措施需要在课程设置、师资教育、学习者教育等方面进行根本性的改变。其中学习者的教育包括学习方法与策略、对教学方法和课堂协议的解读、指引，等等。在课程设置中，教学单位应该采用开放构筑式课程设计(Open Architecture Curricular Design)并重新设计测评方法，侧重于形

成性评估而不是总结性评估。在师资教育中，教学单位可以建立一个理解和实践的社区，树立高期望值，重新设计师资教育，在全校范围内促进获得专业发展的机会。在学习者的教育中，教学单位可以教授学习方法与策略，制定学习者个体化的学习计划，建立（语言能力的）诊断和动态评估档案，以及鼓励学习者在制定学习计划时表达他们的意见。

关键词Keywords: 语言项目; 变革性学习; 变革性语言教学; 开放构筑式课程设计; 形成性评估

超越优秀：如何在四年级俄语课中训练学生达到专业语言水平

越来越多的英语做为二语或外语的专家开始将存在已久的辩论方法融入到外语课堂中，作为学生达到高级语言水平的一种训练方式。事实证明，这样的学习方式有利于培养学生的批判性思维和听说读写能力。本文主要介绍作者们在四年级两门相连的俄语课中使用过的脚手架式教学技巧。在第一门课，俄语421中我们使用时事新闻作为"作案方法modus operandi"，用以教授陈述性演讲，逐步为下一门课，俄语422中进行辩论活动做准备。本文对主要作业设计做了详细叙述。俄语421介绍了每周泛听作业和三个需要课堂口头报告的研究作业。而俄语422则介绍了精读、角色表演、和辩论的作业设计。本文也谈到了四年级俄语课程中短期实习的目的，并讨论了在目标语所在国的时候如何与教学配套以加速所有语言水平的提高。一个使语言学习任务与预期的学习成果相匹配，并提供脚手架教学，让学生不但在课堂上而且在专业环境中完成学习任务的教学设计对连接课堂教学和真实世界中的实际语言运用起到了桥梁作用，并能促进学生的终生学习。

关键词Keywords: 俄罗斯语言, 辩论, 语言能力, 专业, 课程.

The Challenge of the Inverted Pyramid in Attaining Distinguished-Level Proficiency 倒金字塔语言水平递进对获得优异级语言能力的挑战

借鉴于 **Pardee Lowe, Jr.** 1985年的图像表述，本文探讨第二外语学习中从山脚到山顶，追求优异级语言水平能力(**distinguished-level proficiency**) 的攀登之路。优异级语言水平能力指的是接近于母语者的语言水平。追求此成功之路关键取决于两个条件：一是到达大本营，也就是优秀级语言水平能力(**superior-level proficiency**)。二是配备攀登最后高峰所需的设备。为了使获得这种成功的可能性比目前形势更广泛地发生，我们有必要改变众所熟知的倒金字塔对语言能力递进的描述。这反过来要求我们探究这个比喻性结构背后的现实。一旦我们理解了它的本质、形状和原因，前进的道路就会变得更加清晰。实际上，即便我们不能够完全消除障碍，一些特定的教学法和课程设计也可以帮助我们轻装前行。其中之一，开放构筑式课程设计 (**open architecture approach to curriculum design**) 在本文第二部分有描述并假设了一种机制，意在遏制倒金字塔语言水平递进给外语教学带来的挑战。第三部分在对其实质、形状、和坡度进行细查之前，本文作者先对倒金字塔语言水平递进量表的起源和历史进行回顾。最后两个小部分总结了制定倒金字塔语言水平递进量表

的起因以及克服该挑战比较现实的办法（也就是在第二部分中详述的课程设计方法）

Keywords 关键词: **distinguished-level language proficiency**; 优异级语言水平**Interagency Language Roundtable** 跨部门语言圆桌会议; **Level 4 language proficiency** 四级外语水平; **inverted pyramid of proficiency growth** 倒金字塔语言水平递进; **modular curriculum** 模块化课程; **open architecture curricular design** 开放构筑式课程设计

Abstracts in French
Jerôme Collin

Coup d'œil en arrière, regard vers l'avant: Histoire du «Level-4 Movement» et du *Journal for Distinguished Language Studies*

Cet article examine le «Level-4 Movement (mouvement Niveau-4)» d'un point de vue historique: ses débuts au milieu des années 1980, ses plus grandes réalisations vers 2010, sa perte de vitesse au cours des dix années suivantes, et le réengagement actuel d'un petit groupe d'enseignants, apprenants et administrateurs expérimentés et intéressés. Les initiatives de visibilité et de diffusion du mouvement – conférence annuelle, publication des actes de la conférence et parution annuelle d'articles dans le Journal for Distinguished Language Studies, efforts à l'international en association avec la Coalition of Distinguished Language Centres (CDLC) – ont toutes trouvé un terme avec la fermeture du CDLC en 2010. Dans sa partie «regard vers l'avant», l'article suggère que de ces cendres peuvent renaître un phénix, indiquant les domaines où les charbons sont restés chauds, et au sein desquels des individus ont continué à attiser les flammes. Il donne également un aperçu des travaux consacrés aux sujets liés au «Niveau-4», y compris au cours des années 2010-2020.

Mots clés: langue étrangère de niveau très soutenu, histoire du Level-4 movement, Coalition of Distinguished Language Centres, *Journal for Distinguished Language Studies*, publications de niveau 4

Repenser le processus de notation: solution au dilemme de la «performance seuil»

La fiabilité des tests et, intrinsèquement, leur validité sont indiscutablement liées à la validité des critères de notation. Lors de l'évaluation des réponses rédigées dans des tests de haut niveau de compétence linguistique en particulier, l'étendue du niveau de formation et de normalisation des évaluateurs par rapport aux critères et leur capacité à prévoir toutes les réponses éventuellement correctes sont essentielles. Ces problèmes ont une incidence sur les méthodes de normalisation visant à établir deux catégories significatives de candidats qui satisfont et ne satisfont pas aux niveaux de performance minimaux, ce dont va découler la conception et l'objectif du test. La réflexion présentée dans cet article décrit une approche ayant pour but d'établir des barres de seuils dans un test où la compréhension écrite est évaluée par l'expression écrite, mesurant les compétences de compréhension d'un niveau de langue très soutenu par des réponses rédigées. Une approche de méthode mixte est adoptée, dans laquelle les notes globales des évaluateurs sont triangulées avec leurs notes analytiques. La méthode, que les auteurs ont appelée «approche de modélisation rétrodictive» (Retrodictive Modeling Approach, RMA), repose sur le niveau d'expertise et les évaluations globales des évaluateurs, **com**binés avec leur

analyse et leur notation qualitative, ce qui aboutit à un modèle utile pour établir un seuil de niveau de performance. Bien que les allégations de généralisabilité dépassent le cadre de cette étude, des recherches supplémentaires pourraient conduire à une utilisation plus large de la RMA dans les tests de hauts niveaux de compétence.
Journal for Distinguished Language Studies Volume 7 (2011-2020)

Mots clés: établissement de normes; normalisation; validité de la notation, niveaux soutenus

Reconceptualiser les programmes linguistiques pour atteindre le niveau 4

Atteindre le niveau 4 dans la langue cible est un défi en raison de l'étendue et de la profondeur du répertoire linguistique dont doit faire preuve le candidat. Les établissements d'enseignement peuvent mettre en place des mesures éprouvées pour reconcevoir leurs programmes de langue en vue d'atteindre le niveau 4. Les mesures nécessitent un changement fondamental dans la conception des programmes, la formation des enseignants et la formation des apprenants (comprenant ultimement un enseignement des styles et stratégies d'apprentissage pour les apprenants, des orientations sur les approches pédagogiques et des protocoles de classe, etc.). Dans la conception de ses programmes, l'établissement d'enseignement peut adopter la conception de programmes en architecture ouverte et reconcevoir ses évaluations pour se concentrer sur des évaluations formatives plutôt que sommatives. Dans la formation des enseignants, l'établissement peut favoriser une communauté de compréhension et de pratique, fixer des attentes élevées, repenser le programme de formation des enseignants et promouvoir l'accès aux opportunités de développement professionnel à l'échelle de l'institut. Dans le cadre de la formation des apprenants, l'établissement peut fournir des instructions sur les styles et stratégies d'apprentissage, utiliser des plans d'études individualisés, mettre en place un programme de diagnostic et d'évaluation dynamique et promouvoir la voix de l'apprenant.

Mots clés: Programmes linguistiques; Apprentissage transformatif; Apprentissage et enseignement transformatifs des langues; Conception curriculaire en architecture ouverte; évaluation formative

Vers un niveau supérieur et au-delà : développer des compétences professionnelles dans un programme russe de quatrième année

Un nombre croissant de spécialistes dans le domaine de l'enseignement des langues secondes et étrangères commence à intégrer la tradition – ancienne et bien établie – des débats dans les classes de langue étrangère comme moyen d'atteindre des niveaux élevés de compétence. Une telle approche s'est avérée bénéfique pour le développement de la pensée critique et des quatre compétences linguistiques. Cet article traite d'un certain nombre de techniques pédagogiques employées dans deux cours consécutifs de quatrième année de langue russe, dont le premier (cours

421) utilise l'actualité comme modus operandi pour enseigner le discours de type «présentation», en préparation du deuxième cours (cours 422) qui donne à celui-ci une portée opérationnelle dans le cadre de l'exercice rhétorique culminant qu'est le débat. Une description détaillée des tâches principales est fournie, qui pour le cours 421 comprend des travaux d'écoute hebdomadaires et trois projets de recherche qui aboutissent à des présentations en classe, et pour le cours 422: lecture intensive, jeux de rôle et débats. L'article aborde également l'objectif des stages dans le programme de russe de quatrième année et comprend une discussion sur la façon dont le temps passé dans le pays, associé à un enseignement adapté au besoin linguistique, accélère l'acquisition de compétences à tous les niveaux. Un programme qui aligne les tâches d'apprentissage avec les résultats de compétence recherchés et qui fournit un appareil d'activités pédagogique pour accomplir ces tâches à la fois en classe et dans un cadre professionnel sert à relier l'enseignement formel des langues avec son application dans le monde réel, et contribue à un apprentissage capable de se poursuivre tout au long de la vie.

Mots clés: langue russe, débat, maîtrise de la langue, professionnel, programme.

Le défi de la pyramide inversée pour atteindre un niveau de haute maîtrise linguistique

S'appuyant sur les métaphores d'une contribution de Pardee Lowe, Jr. datant de 1985, cet article envisage la quête de compétence de niveau «Distinguished-L2» comme l'ascension conduisant du pied d'une montagne à son sommet (compétence quasi-native ou niveau de haute maîtrise linguistique). Le succès de cette quête dépend essentiellement de deux conditions: (1) atteindre le camp de base (correspondant en quelque sorte à la compétence de niveau avancé) avec suffisamment d'avance, et (2) posséder l'équipement nécessaire pour l'ascension finale. Pour que cela puisse e se produire avec une meilleure probabilité de réussite qu'aujourd'hui, il est nécessaire de vaincre d'une manière ou d'une autre le phénomène connu sous le nom de «pyramide inversée». Cela nous oblige alors à sonder la réalité qui sous-tend cette construction métaphorique. Une fois que nous comprenons sa nature, sa forme et ses causes, la voie à suivre devient plus claire, et il existe de fait des approches de conception pédagogique et curriculaire spécifiques qui peuvent nous aider à l'atténuer, voire à l'éliminer complètement. L'une d'entre elles – approche modulaire d'architecture ouverte dans la conception des programmes – est décrite dans la section 2, et une hypothèse est formulée quant au mécanisme par lequel elle semble atténuer le phénomène de la pyramide inversée. La section 3 examine l'origine et l'histoire de la structure pyramidale inversée avant de passer à un examen de sa substance, de sa forme et de sa pente. Les deux dernières sous-sections résument les causes du phénomène de la pyramide inversée et les approches réalistes pour le vaincre, qui incluent l'approche curriculaire décrite dans la section 2.

Mots clés : pyramide inversée de la croissance des compétences ; conception de programmes d'architecture ouverte (OACD) ; curriculum modulaire ; Haute maîtrise de la langue ; Interagency Language Roundtable Level 4 language proficiency

Abstracts in Russian
Irene Krasner

Взгляд назад, взгляд вперед: история «движения языкового четвертого уровня» и журнал исследований продвинутого уровня

В этой статье, с исторической точки зрения рассматривается, так называемое "движение четвертого языкого уровня", которое, начиная с середины 1980-х годов до примерно 2010-ого году, когда оно достигло своего расцвета, и постепенно ослабевая в течение следующих десяти лет, достигло нынешнего периода, и возродилось, благодаря усилиям небольшой группы опытных и заинтересованных преподавателей, учащихся и администраторов. Механизмы распространения этого движения, а именно, ежегодная конференция, публикация трудов конференций и ежегодное появление статей в журнале языковых исследований продвинутого уровня, а так же международное контакты, связанные с Коалицией языковых центров продвинутого уровня (CDLC) – все это исчезло в связи с закрытием CDLC в 2010 года. В части этой статьи, озаглавленной «Взгляд вперед» утверждается, что из тлеющих углей предыдущей работы как феникс может это движение возродиться, и указываются те места, где "угли еще горячие", и тех людей, которые "продолжают их раздувать". Также в статье представлен обзор работ, посвященных темам продвинутого уровня, в том числе работ 2010-2020 годов.

Ключевые слова: иностранный язык продвинутого уровня, история движения четвертого уровня, коалиция в языковых центров, журнал языковых исследований продвинутого уровня, и публикации четвертого уровня.

Переосмысление использования критериев процесса оценки в тестировании: решение дилеммы порогового уровня владения языком

Надежность исследований и, конечно, их валидность имеют неоспоримую связь с действующими критериями оценки. При оценке сконструированных ответов, в частности, в тестах на очень продвинутый уровень владения языком, решающее значение имеют уровень подготовки экзаменаторов и как они следуют критериям, а также их способность предвидеть все возможные правильные ответы. Эти вопросы имеют отношение к методам установления стандартов, направленных на определение двух различных категорий кандидатов: тех, которые соответствуют минимальным критериям уровня владения языком, и тех, которые не соответствуют этим критериям, что является сутью концепции тестирования и отражают его цель. В этом концептуальном документе описывается подход к установлению нижнего предела шкалы в интегрированном тесте на понимание прочитанного посредством навыка письма, который предназначен для измерения продвинутых навыков чтения с помощью вопросов и "открытых" ответов. Применяется смешанный метод, при котором целостный подход экзаменаторов триангулируются с их аналитическими оценками. Метод, который авторы назвали подходом к ретро-моделированию (РМП), основывается на уровне знаний экзаменаторов и целостной оценки в сочетании с их качественным анализом и оценками, которые дают образец, полезный для установления порогового уровня эффективности. Хотя заявления о возможности обобщения выходят за рамки данного исследования, дальнейшие исследования могут привести к более широкому использованию РМПА в тестах на продвинутый уровень квалификации. Журнал выдающихся исследований продвинутого уровня языка, том 7 (2011-2020).

Ключевые слова: стандартная установка; нормирование; оценка достоверности, продвинутые уровни

Переосмысление языковых программ для достижения уровня 4

Достижение четвертого уровня изучаемого языка является сложной задачей из-за большого объема и глубины языкового репертуара, который должен быть продемонстрирован учащимся. Для переосмысления своих языковых программ с целью достижения уровня 4 учебные заведения могут применять уже проверенные способы работы. Но эти способы потребуют фундаментальных изменений в структуре учебных программ, педагогическом образовании и обучении учащихся (последнее включает обучение стилям и стратегиям учащихся, ориентацию на педагогические подходы протокол занятий и т. д.). При разработке учебного плана учебное заведение может принять дизайн учебного плана с открытой архитектурой и изменить дизайн экзаменов, чтобы сосредоточиться на формирующих, а не на итоговых тестах. В педагогическом образовании учебное заведение может способствовать формированию сообщества взаимопонимания и практики, устанавливать высокие критерии, пересматривать программу обучения учителей и содействовать доступу к возможностям профессионального развития в масштабе всего института. В сфере обучения учащихся учебное заведение может предоставить инструкции по стилю и стратегии обучения, использовать индивидуальные учебные планы, создать диагностическую и динамическую программу оценки знаний и учитывать мнение учащегося.

Ключевые слова: языковые программы; преобразующее обучение; трансформативное изучение и преподавание языков; газработка учебных программ по открытой архитектуре; формирующая оценка.

Продвинутый уровень и выше: достижения профессионального уровня владения языком на четвертом курсе программы русского языка

Все большее количество специалистов в области ESL/EFL начинают внедрять давнюю традицию дебатов в классы иностранного языка как способ достижения высокого уровня владения языком. Такой подход оказался полезным для развития критического мышления и общих навыков говорения, чтения, аудирования и письма. В этой статье рассматривается ряд строительных педагогических приемов, используемых в двух последовательных четырехлетних курсах русского языка, первый из которых (русский 421) использует текущие события в качестве метода обучения презентационной речи при подготовке ко второму курсу (русский 422). это операционализирует презентационную речь в кульминационном риторическом упражнении дискуссии. Дается подробное описание основных задач, которые для русского языка 421 включают еженедельные обширные задания по аудированию и три исследовательских проекта, которые завершаются презентациями в классе, а для русского языка 422 - интенсивное чтение, ролевые игры и дебаты. В статье также рассматривается цель стажировок в русской учебной программе четвертого года обучения и обсуждается, как время, проведенное в стране в сочетании с обучением на соответствующем уровне языка, ускоряет получение знаний на всех уровнях. Учебная программа, которая сопоставляет учебные задачи с желаемыми результатами обучения и обеспечивает основу для выполнения этих задач как в классе, так и в профессиональной среде, служит для объединения формального языкового обучения с реальным применением и способствует обучению на протяжении всей жизни.

Ключевые слова: русский язык, дебаты, владение языком, профессиональный, учебная программа.

Трудности приложения "перевернутой пирамиды" для достижения продвинутого лингвистического уровня

Основываясь на графиках из выступления Парди Лоу-младшего в 1985 году, эта статья описывает процесс поиска достижения продвинутого уровня владения иностранным языком как восхождение от подножия горы к вершине (к уровню практически равному носителя языка, иначе говоря к продвинотому уровню). Успех в этом квесте в решающей степени зависит от двух условий: (1) достижения "базового лагеря" (с навыками высшего уровня) за определенное время и (2) "наличие оборудования", необходимого для финального восхождения. Чтобы это могло произойти в более широком масштабе, чем сейчас, необходимо каким-то образом преодолетъ явление, известное как "перевернутая пирамида". Это, в свою очередь, требует от нас исследования сути этой метафорической конструкции. Как только мы поймем ее природу, форму и причины, путь к достижению цели станет более ясным. На самом деле существуют конкретные подходы к обучению и разработке учебных программ, которые могут помочь нам смягчить, если не полностью устранить трудности, связанные с этим явление . Один из них, модульный подход с открытой архитектурой к разработке учебных программ, описан в разделе 2, где сформулирована гипотеза механизма, с помощью которого, по-видимому, можно смягчитъ феномен "перевернутой пирамиды". В разделе 3 рассматривается происхождение и история конструкции "перевернутой пирамиды", а затем исследование ее содержания, формы и угла наклона. В последних двух подразделах суммируются причины феномена "перевернутой пирамиды" и реалистичные подходы к ее освоению, включая учебный подход, описанный в разделе 2.

Ключевые слова: перевернутая пирамида языкового роста; разработка учебных программ по открытой архитектуре (OACD); модульная учебная программа; знание языка на высшем уровне; межведомственный круглый стол по языкам знание языка уровня 4

Abstracts in Spanish
R. Txabarriaga

Una mirada al pasado, una mirada al futuro: la historia del "Movimiento del Nivel 4" y los anales JDLS

En este artículo se examina desde una perspectiva histórica el denominado "Movimiento del Nivel 4", que empezó a mediados de la década de 1980 y alcanzó sus mayores logros alrededor de 2010. Aunque se desvaneció lentamente en la siguiente década, en la actualidad ha revivido gracias a un pequeño grupo de educadores, estudiantes y administradores con experiencia e interés en su continuidad. Entre los mecanismos de socialización del movimiento, labor internacional asociada con la Coalición de Centros de Idiomas de Nivel Distinguido (Coalition of Distinguished Language Centers, CDLC), se encontraban un congreso anual, la publicación de las presentaciones de dicho congreso y la inclusión de artículos en los Anales para Estudios de Idiomas de Nivel Distinguido (Journal for Distinguished Language Studies, JDLS). Tales mecanismos habían prácticamente desaparecido tras el cierre del CDLC en 2010. Al "mirar al futuro", en este artículo se sugiere que de las brasas puede surgir un ave fénix, y se indican los lugares en los que la llama sigue viva y las personas responsables de alimentar el fuego. También se ofrece un resumen de obras dedicadas a temas del Nivel 4, incluidas las de la década de 2010.

Palabras clave: idioma extranjero a nivel distinguido, historia del movimiento del Nivel 4, Coalition of Distinguished Language Centers, *Journal for Distinguished Language Studies*, publicaciones sobre el Nivel 4

Repensar el proceso de calificación: una solución al dilema del rendimiento mínimo

La fiabilidad de las pruebas, y por ende su validez, están indudablemente conectadas a criterios válidos de puntuación. Al evaluar respuestas de constructo, específicamente en pruebas de nivel de fluidez en un idioma a niveles muy avanzados, son esenciales el nivel de formación del evaluador, lo estandarizado de los criterios de calificación, y la capacidad de anticipar todas las posibles respuestas correctas. Estos temas influyen en los métodos empleados para establecer estándares, los cuales tienen por objetivo definir dos categorías principales de los candidatos que cumplen y los que no cumplen los niveles mínimos frente a los criterios de rendimiento. Estos niveles ejemplifican el constructo y reflejan el propósito de la prueba. En este artículo conceptual se describe un enfoque para establecer las puntuaciones mínimas en una prueba integrada de comprensión de lectura a través de destrezas de redacción, con la intención de medir las destrezas de lectura a un nivel de fluidez distinguido mediante respuestas de constructo. Se adopta un enfoque de método combinado en el que el cálculo de las calificaciones integrales de los evaluadores se efectúa con las puntuaciones analíticas. El método, que los autores han denominado Enfoque de modelado retrodictivo (Retrodictive Modeling Approach, RMA), se vale del nivel de experiencia de los evaluadores y las calificaciones integrales, junto con su análisis cualitativo y puntuaciones, para producir un patrón que sea útil al establecer un nivel mínimo de rendimiento. Aunque los argumentos en torno al potencial de generalización se apartan del alcance de este estudio, más investigación podría llevar a un uso más extenso del RMA en pruebas de fluidez a nivel distinguido. *Journal for Distinguished Language Studies, Volumen 7* (2011-2020).

Palabras clave: estructura estándar; normalización; validez de puntuación, niveles distinguidos de fluidez

Reconceptualizar los programas de idiomas para alcanzar el Nivel 4 de fluidez

Alcanzar el Nivel 4 de fluidez en un idioma extranjero es un reto debido al gran alcance y profundidad de repertorio lingüístico que el candidato debe demostrar. Las instituciones de aprendizaje pueden implementar medidas comprobadas para reconceptualizar sus programas de idiomas y alcanzar el Nivel 4. Las medidas requieren cambios fundamentales en diseño de currículo y en la formación de profesores y estudiantes (para estos últimos se incluye la enseñanza de estilos y estrategias de aprendizaje, orientación sobre enfoques pedagógicos y protocolo para el aula, etc.). Al diseñar currículo, la institución de aprendizaje puede adoptar un diseño de estructura abierta y modificar las evaluaciones de manera tal que se centren en evaluaciones formativas en lugar de sumativas. En cuanto a la formación de profesores, la institución puede fomentar una comunidad de comprensión y práctica, establecer expectativas altas, rediseñar el programa de formación de profesores y promover el acceso a oportunidades de desarrollo profesional en toda la institución. Respecto a la formación del estudiante, la institución puede ofrecer clases sobre estilos y estrategias de aprendizaje, usar planes de estudio individualizados, implementar un programa de evaluaciones de diagnóstico que sea dinámico y promover la voz del estudiante.

Palabras clave: programas de idiomas; aprendizaje transformativo; aprendizaje y enseñanza transformativa de idiomas; diseño curricular de estructura abierta; evaluación formativa

Hacia el Nivel superior y más allá: Desarrollo de fluidez profesional en un programa de cuarto año de ruso

Cada vez más especialistas en los campos de ESL y EFL están empezando a integrar la tradición de larga data de sostener discusiones en el aula de idioma extranjero como forma de alcanzar altos niveles de fluidez. Se ha demostrado que este enfoque da resultados para el desarrollo de razonamiento analítico y destrezas generales para hablar, leer, escuchar y escribir. En este artículo se abordan varias técnicas pedagógicas de andamiaje utilizadas en dos cursos consecutivos de cuarto año de ruso. En el primero de tales cursos (ruso 421) se utilizan eventos de actualidad como modus operandi para la enseñanza de oratoria y a modo de preparación para el segundo curso (ruso 422), en el cual se pone en práctica la oratoria en el ejercicio retórico final de sostener discusiones en grupo. En el artículo se incluye una descripción detallada de las principales tareas, que para el curso de ruso 421 incluyen extensos deberes semanales centrados en escuchar y tres proyectos de investigación que culminan con presentaciones ante la clase, mientras que para ruso 422 se usan con intensidad la lectura, las representaciones y las discusiones en grupo. En el artículo también se aborda el objetivo de tener pasantías en el currículo de cuarto año de ruso y se incluye un análisis de la forma en que pasar tiempo en el país del idioma extranjero, junto con la enseñanza adecuada para el nivel, aceleran el aumento de la fluidez en todos los niveles. Un currículo en el que se alinean las tareas de aprendizaje con los resultados deseados en cuanto a la fluidez, y que además suministra el andamiaje para llevar a cabo tales tareas tanto en el aula como en entornos profesionales, sirve para vincular la enseñanza formal de idiomas con la práctica en el mundo real y contribuye al aprendizaje de por vida.

El desafío de la pirámide invertida para lograr la fluidez a nivel distinguido

En este artículo se utilizan como base las imágenes presentadas en una contribución de Pardee Lowe, Jr. en 1985 para enmarcar la misión hacia la fluidez a Nivel distinguido L2 en forma del ascenso a una montaña desde la falda hasta la cima (fluidez cercana a lengua materna o a nivel distinguido). El éxito de la misión depende fundamentalmente de dos condiciones: (1) llegar al campamento base (aproximadamente la fluidez a nivel superior) con tiempo suficiente y, (2) con los equipos necesarios para el ascenso final. Para mejorar la probabilidad de que esto ocurra de manera más generalizada que en la actualidad, es necesario superar de alguna manera el fenómeno conocido como pirámide invertida. Esto requiere a la vez la investigación de la realidad en el trasfondo de este constructo metafórico. Cuando se consigue comprender su carácter, su forma y sus causas, el camino por recorrer es más definido y se crean de hecho enfoques de diseño instructivo y de currículo que pueden ayudar a mitigar, e incluso a eliminar completamente la pirámide invertida. Uno de tales enfoques consiste en abordar el diseño de currículo como una estructura abierta y modular. Este se describe en la Sección 2, y se presenta una hipótesis como uno de los mecanismos que parecen mitigar el fenómeno de la pirámide invertida. En la Sección 3 se analizan el origen y la historia de la pirámide invertida antes de pasar a examinar su esencia, su forma y su pendiente. En los dos apartados finales se resumen las causas del fenómeno de la pirámide invertida y enfoques realistas para superarla, entre los que se incluyen el enfoque curricular descrito en la Sección 2.

BOOK REVIEW

Dictionary of Advanced Russian Usage, Second Edition
Michael Kayser, Schreiber Publishing, 2020, 844 pages

Jack Franke

Imagine the opportunity to sit with a contracted State Department simultaneous interpreter and an American Translator Association-certified translator—a person who is a Russian-language expert with decades of experience unweaving the nuances and subtleties between Russian and English. How much would a student pay for an hour of tutoring from such an experienced person? For the price of a couple of drinks, a Russian student can receive hundreds—if not thousands—of hours of knowledge and enjoyment in the 2nd edition of Kayser's *Dictionary of Advanced Russian Usage* (DARU). DARU 2.0 is an 844-page compilation of one man's pursuit of Russian language mastery, with roughly twice the content of the first edition. His painstaking efforts at transcribing his journals and experiences have resulted in this incredible tome.

To best understand the premise of this book, the reader should know what this book is not. DARU 2.0 is not intended to replace a general dictionary like Katzner's, Oxford's, or Google Translate. The strengths in this dictionary are the contextual examples and sample sentences. Kayser draws on a wide swath of literature, life experiences, and specialized references to encompass the book.

Other aspects of DARU 2.0 include slang and collocations. Take the word 'nose,' for example. Kayser provides dozens of examples like beak, snoot, schnoz, snot-locker, and schnozzola. In addition, the author gives 'to have a runny nose,' 'as clear as the nose on your face,' 'to have a nose for something,' 'to have one's nose to the grindstone,' and 'nose to nose' (p. 362). DARU 2.0 delves into the intricacies of addressing the word "ain't" with a whole page of examples, the drug culture (i.e., "to shoot up," "to get high," etc.), as well as drinking in the Russian culture. Moreover, Kayser dedicates two pages (pp. 247-248) to the concept of "hangover" in addition to tricky words like "whistle-blower," "to play hardball," "bat-shit crazy," "awesome," and over a 1000 entries of criminal kant.

In summary, Kayser's *Dictionary of Advanced Russian Usage* 2.0 is 844 pages of sheer enjoyment, akin to drawing water from a never-ending well. Whether you wish to shock native Russian speakers with spot-on translations or raise your proficiency to the next level, this book is for you. I recommend this dictionary for all intermediate and advanced learners of Russian.

Professor Jack Franke, Ph.D., is at the Defense Language Institute Foreign Language Center in Monterey, California.

GENERAL INFORMATION

Books about Distinguished Language Proficiency Published in 2011-2020

Brown, T., T. Balykhina, E. Talalakina, J. Bown, & E. Kurilenko. 2014
Mastering Russian through Global Debate
Washington, DC: Georgetown University Press

Mastering Russian through Global Debate brings together the rhetorical traditions of the communications field and the best practices of adult second language instruction to facilitate superior-level proficiency in the Russian language. Each chapter addresses a rich topic of debate, providing students with a set of prereading activities, texts covering both sides of a debate topic, and continues with postreading comprehension and lexical development exercises—all of which foster the language and critical thinking skills needed for successful debates. A rhetorical methods section in each chapter integrates language and practice and prepares students for end-of-chapter debates. Using debate to develop advanced competency in a second language is a method that is finding increased interest among instructors and students alike, in both synchronous online teaching and the individual classroom. Students are prepared to participate fully in debates with their classmates—at home, abroad, or both. While intended for use at Advanced and Superior levels, the exercises can inform programs for Distinguished-level learning as well.

Brown, T., & Bown, J. 2015
To Advanced Proficiency and Beyond:
Theory and Methods for Developing Superior Second Language Ability
Washington, DC: Georgetown University Press

This book addresses an important issue in Second Language Acquisition—how to help learners progress from Intermediate and Advanced proficiency to Superior and beyond. Due to the pressures of globalization, American society encounters an ever-increasing demand for speakers with advanced language abilities. This volume makes available cutting edge research on working memory and cognition and empirical studies of effective teaching. In addition, it can serve as a practical handbook for seasoned and pre-professional instructors alike. The bringing together of the latest in second language acquisition theory, decades of empirical research, and practical classroom application makes for an unprecedented volume examining the achievement of Superior-level foreign language proficiency.

Brown, T., & Bown, J. 2016
Teaching Advanced Language Skills through Global Debate: Theory and Practice
Washington, DC: Georgetown University Press

Using debate to develop advanced competency in a second language is a method that is finding increased interest among instructors and students alike, whether in synchronous online 2teaching or the individual classroom. Through debate, students learn how to make hypotheses, support their conclusions with evidence, and deploy the rhetoric of persuasion in the target language. Though this method provides an exciting pedagogy for moving students from the advanced to the superior level, there is a paucity of materials available for instructors who wish to plan a curriculum focused on debate. Teaching Advanced Language Skills through Global Debate: Theory and Practice provides teachers with both the theoretical underpinnings for using debate in the foreign language classroom as well as practical advice for developing reading, listening, writing, and speaking skills through debate. It discusses task-based language learning and helps instructors design debate-related tasks for the classroom. While the focus is on lower levels—Advanced and Superior—the practices proposed can be adapted for teaching at the Distinguished level.

Shekhtman, B. S., ed. 2016
How to Use Your Russian in Communication Effectively
CreateSpace

The book presents language models, texts, and exercises at Levels 1-4, moving learners steadily along from lower levels to high levels. There are 84 models at the Distinguished level. Written by experts at teaching at Level 4.

Shekhtman, B. S., & Kupchanka, D. 2015
Communicative Focus: Teaching Foreign Languages on the Basis of the Native Speaker's Communicative Focus.
Virginia Beach, VA; Villa Magna, LLC

In *Communicative Focus*, Boris Shekhtman describes in detail the principles and practices used in his approach to language teaching. He is not afraid to talk about some aspects of language learning and teaching, such as the development of lexical and grammatical accuracy, as well as the need for memorization and the development of memory, that have been increasingly omitted from the classroom as a result of the rise in popularity of theories that debase their significance but which are very important, especially if students are to reach the highest level of proficiency. He also discusses some ideas, such as the unique nature of the connection between language and meaning that native speakers experience that non-native speakers must learn to deal with-in differing ways at differing levels of proficiency. His focus throughout is on communication and the nature of communicative focus (and its development). Just as many students have tremendously benefited from Boris's unique approach to language teaching, many teachers can benefit from the information he has included in this book if they put aside their graduate-school-enforced understandings of how foreign-language development can occur if looked at from a point of view that we have not generally taken in the past. I recommend to all teachers who want to see leaps in their students' progress in developing language proficiency and who are willing to take upon themselves (as opposed to leaving to students) much of the responsibility for language acquisition to read this book carefully and to return to it frequently.

Talalakina, E., T. Brown, J. Bown, & W. Eggington. 2015
Mastering English through Global Debate
Washington, DC: Georgetown University Press

Mastering English through Global Debate brings together rhetorical traditions and the best practices of ESL instruction to facilitate superior-level proficiency in the English language. Each chapter addresses a rich topic of debate, providing students with a set of prereading activities, texts covering both sides of a debate topic, and post-reading comprehension and lexical development exercises—all of which foster the language and critical thinking skills needed for successful debates. A rhetorical methods section in each chapter integrates language and practice and prepares students for end-of-chapter debates. Using debate to develop advanced competency in a second language is a method that is finding increased interest among instructors and students alike, in both synchronous online teaching and the individual classroom. Students are prepared to participate fully in debates with their classmates—at home, abroad, or both. While intended for use at Advanced and Superior levels, the exercises can inform programs for Distinguished-level learning as well.

Williams, P. (2018)
Advanced Writing Skills for Students of English
UK (online): Brighton English Lessons

Want to know how to write better in English? How do you make your message clear and easy to understand? How do you vary your sentences and vocabulary to keep readers engaged? How do you use advanced language without being confusing? The answers to these questions and more can be found in *Advanced Writing Skills for Students of English.* Through discussing wide range of topics, Phil Williams presents a series of tips for better writing with a focus on analyzing the grammatical rules and reasoning behind each.

This guide also looks, in brief, at the considerations required for specific areas of writing. Writing is a skill that takes time and personal practice to master, and Phil Williams' latest language guide is a simply-presented aide to start you on that journey today.

Call for Papers

Journal for Distinguished Language Studies, Volume 8: 2021
A refereed journal

Editors

- Editor, Yalun Zhou, Ph.D., Rensselaer Polytechnic Institute, New York, USA
- Assistant Editor, Donna Bain Butler, Ph.D., Delaware State University, Delaware, USA

Advisory Board

- Dr. Rajai Al-Khanji, University of Jordan
- Dr. Andrew Corin, Defense Language Institute (Emeritus)
- Dr. Rebecca Oxford, University of Alabama at Birmingham
- Dr. Karin Ryding, Georgetown University (Emerita)
- Dr. Nelleke Van Deusen-Scholle, Yale University

Overview

The *Journal for Distinguished Language Studies* (JDLS), founded by the Coalition of Distinguished Language Centers under the direction of Dr. Betty Lou Leaver and Boris Shekhtman in 2002 is a refereed volume and the only journal to focus exclusively on the highest levels of language achievement, that is, native-like or near-native. This level is labeled Distinguished by the American Council on the Teaching of Foreign Languages (ACTFL), *Level 4/Advanced Professional Proficiency* by the Interagency Language Roundtable (ILR), and also Level 4 as part of the Standardized Agreement (STANAG) 6001 of NATO's Bureau of International Language Co-ordination (BILC). Descriptions can be found at the ACTFL, ILR, and BILC websites.

The purpose of this journal is to create a robust international movement to promote and support language learning to the near-native level of proficiency. The editors are seeking contributions in the areas of theory, research, and applications. The journal typically has published a balance of articles in all three categories. Published papers will thus develop theory, share applications that work (based on the experience of those who teach that level), and report on the research conducted and needed for proper evaluation and assessment of theory and application.

We particularly welcome articles on the following areas:

- **current status of Level 4 proficiency research in each of the four skill areas;**
- teaching methods to/at/above Level 4 proficiency in each of the four skill areas;
- the role of culture in achieving Level 4 proficiency in each of the four skill areas; and
- assessment to/at/above Level 4 proficiency in each of the four skill areas.

Submissions should represent original work. They should not have been previously published elsewhere nor be currently submitted to another journal or collected volume.

Submission Process and Deadlines

- Please submit (5,000-8,000 Word doc.) articles by June 30, 2020. Include paper title (10 words max.), abstract (200-250 words max.), affiliation, and one blind copy (omitting the name and institutional affiliation of the author at the beginning of the article). Blinded articles will be sent to reviewers.
- Use *Publication Manual of the American Psychological Association, Seventh Edition.*
- Because journal articles are now English only, please ensure that a native speaker/proficient writer proofreads prior to submission so peer review can focus on content. The editors reserve the right to return, without review, any articles that are not clear, accurate, or concise (i.e. Level 4 writing proficiency).
- We expect to receive reviewers' recommendations by August 1, immediately after which we will let potential contributors know whether the manuscript has been accepted, needs revision, or has been rejected. We will need to receive revised manuscripts no later than October 31, 2020.
- Publication is anticipated for December 2021, with galleys available for proofreading in November.
- Potential authors may contact the editors in advance with any questions.

Request specs from/submit articles to: Dr. Yalun Zhou (zhouy12@rpi.edu)
  Copy: Dr. Donna Bain Butler (dbutler@desu.edu)

www.ingramcontent.com/pod-product-compliance
Lightning Source LLC
Chambersburg PA
CBHW061129010526
44117CB00023B/2996